TASTING
ROME

TASTING
ROME

FRESH FLAVORS & FORGOTTEN RECIPES
FROM AN ANCIENT CITY

Katie Parla and Kristina Gill

CLARKSON POTTER/PUBLISHERS
NEW YORK

Copyright © 2016 by Katie Parla
and Kristina Gill
Photographs copyright © 2016
by Kristina Gill

Published in the United States by Clarkson
Potter/Publishers, an imprint of the Crown
Publishing Group,
a division of Penguin Random House LLC,
New York.
www.crownpublishing.com
www.clarksonpotter.com

Library of Congress Cataloging-in-
Publication Data
Parla, Katie.
   Tasting Rome : fresh flavors and
forgotten recipes from an ancient city /
Katie Parla and Kristina Gill—First edition.
     pages   cm
   Includes bibliographical references and
index.
1. Cooking, Italian. 2. Cooking—Italy—
Rome. I. Gill, Kristina. II. Title.
   TX723.P344 2016
   641.5937—dc23   2015023715

ISBN 978-0-8041-8718-3
eBook ISBN 978-0-8041-8719-0

Printed in China

Cover and book design by
Stephanie Huntwork
Cover photographs by Kristina Gill
Back cover and title page illustration (wolf)
by Meighan Cavanaugh
Photographs on pages 2, 48 (top left, top
right, bottom left),172–173, 177, 180, 183,
196, and 199 by Matt Armendariz

10 9 8

First Edition

For Mamma Parla, Papa Parla,
Lauren Parla, Nonno Cipollina, and Chris Behr

—KATIE PARLA

For my father, my biggest fan

—KRISTINA GILL

CONTENTS

INTRODUCTION

There's a huge field in the center of Rome. It used to be a stadium
called the Circus Maximus and chariots raced around its half-mile
circumference in front of a quarter million fans. Now it's a sort
of dusty, neglected dog park. It hosts the occasional jogger. Kids
cutting class recline on the slopes where the bleachers used to
be. Sometimes tourists picnic in the shade of the umbrella pines
planted at the end of the field beside a converted pasta factory
where the city's Opera builds and stores its sets.

It's spots like this one that make us love Rome. The cobblestoned streets, baroque fountains, pastel palaces, and lively piazzas have obvious appeal. They're easy to love, but we're more drawn to the city's surreal bits like the pasta-factory-turned-opera-warehouse next to a giant ruin. Rome is full of similar contrasts, places where contemporary life proceeds normally in spite of extraordinary or sometimes bizarre settings.

So how did two Americans end up in this strangely beautiful and beguiling ancient city? Our roads to the Italian capital were a bit different. Katie, a New Jersey native, came in 2003 as a recent college graduate with an art history degree. She planned to continue studying art but was immediately distracted by the local cuisine; she turned her attention to food instead and earned a master's degree in Italian gastronomic culture at the Università degli Studi di Roma "Tor Vergata." Kristina was transferred to Rome in 1999 for work, after having studied for a year in Florence as an undergraduate and a year in Bologna as a graduate student. Neither of us ever left. Katie now works as a freelance food and beverage journalist, culinary guide, and lecturer, while Kristina is the food and drinks editor at Design*Sponge, a freelance photographer, and a development adviser focused on food assistance. We may have arrived here with other plans, but Rome's food and drinks won us over for good.

When our paths finally merged, we found that our experiences exploring Rome—Katie for food research, Kristina for photography—shared a lot of common ground. We both loved documenting Rome's lost recipes and contemporary innovations and were eager to share dishes and stories that only a fully immersed Rome dweller could know. We enjoyed celebrating new flavors and breaking down the stereotype that Roman food must be hypertraditional in order to be authentic. Most of all, we loved using food as a vehicle for providing a complete picture of our adopted city.

While crafting this book, we sought inspiration in peripheral, graffiti-clad neighborhoods, patrician districts, archeological parks, neighborhood bakeries, artisanal gelato shops, dimly lit cocktail bars, chaotic markets, and innovative restaurants. The result of our explorations is this collection of recipes that embraces Roman flavors and goes beyond the tight focus on tradition to acknowledge that the city's cuisine has evolved and that strict tradition, while predominant, certainly isn't the only reality.

rome: then and now

Before we can start talking about what we eat in Rome today, we have to step back about three thousand years to see where it all comes from. Of course, there are plenty of modern tools and New World ingredients in Roman kitchens today and the cuisine continues to evolve from its origins, but many of those flavors we know as distinctly Roman have been on local tables since the beginning.

Rome has always been bound to its rural origins—the city's founding father, Romulus, was a shepherd, after all. According to legend, Rome was founded on April 21, 753 BC. On that date, Romulus, the son of the god Mars and nearby royalty, killed his twin brother, Remus, and became the first king of a simple settlement.

Romulus, for whom the city is named, was succeeded by six other kings, some of Etruscan stock. The Etruscans were a sophisticated trading society eventually overcome by the Romans, but not before imparting their engineering and viticultural prowess upon the primitive Roman sheepherders.

This kingdom was followed by the Republic, an oligarchy established in 509 BC, which was ruled by wealthy families. During its nearly five centuries under Republican rule, Rome was transformed from a malarial backwater into a thriving city with a complex infrastructure and vast, suburban farm estates. As the city grew and its territories expanded, it demanded additional nourishment. Grand aqueducts were built to supply the Romans with fresh water (a similar system still feeds modern Rome). The conquest of southern Italy and North Africa paved the way for state-sponsored grain cultivation in those zones, which was bolstered by a robust commercial network and near-complete dominance of the Mediterranean.

By the time the first emperor, Augustus, took the throne in 27 BC, Rome was a burgeoning capital with nearly 1 million residents living in an area that corresponds to today's historical center (currently inhabited by fewer than 123,000). Romans imported spices, wine, condiments, and olive oil, and the patrician class entertained itself with elaborate banquets showcasing exotic produce and game meat. Meanwhile, the urban poor lived mainly on cereals, legumes, porridge, and bread, and many relied on state rations or upper-class generosity for food.

The decline and fall of the Roman Empire saw the city return to its agricultural roots. By the fifth century, the population had plummeted and Rome, once the command center for a vast empire, was reduced to a handful of small villages separated by livestock pastures and swamps.

From around 600 BC until AD 1870, with only brief interruptions, popes ruled Rome. Monasteries and convents operated vineyards and farms. The Crusades momentarily brought Rome out of relative isolation and in contact with the East and its spice trade, but for the most part, the city's medieval diet remained simple and relied on locally cultivated produce, legumes, and lamb, all of which still play an important part in today's cuisine.

When the Roman Renaissance began in the mid-fifteenth century, wealth returned to noble tables, while peasants ate simple, rural cuisine and small taverns catered to pilgrims. The subsequent Baroque era brought lavish banquets, naturally reserved for the upper class. Meanwhile, from 1555 until 1870, the popes confined Rome's Jews to a squalid, flood-prone Ghetto, where isolation, poverty, sumptuary laws, and the rules of Kashrut gave rise to a unique cuisine called the *cucina ebraica romanesca* (page 105).

In 1870, after twelve centuries of papal rule, Rome fell to a secular unification movement led by King Vittorio Emanuele II and General Giuseppe Garibaldi. The Ghetto was liberated and Rome began its tremendous transformation from a dilapidated, insalubrious swamp into a flourishing European capital. For the next century, migrants from every corner of Italy converged on the city to build river embankments, factories, housing, and public works. The population swelled and peasants from Abruzzo, Calabria, Campania, Sicily, and elsewhere brought their culture and traditions, all influencing the local cuisine, called the *cucina romana*, as they assimilated.

Cucina romana refers to Roman cooking as a whole. Ironically, outsiders have had a strong influence—particularly peasants arriving from impoverished rural regions from 1870 to 1970. Local cuisine has been infiltrated fabulously by ingredients, customs, and techniques also inherited from laborers, bureaucrats, and students arriving from other parts of Italy. Their regional Italian elements mingled with native traditions to produce the Roman classics, and the transformation is ongoing.

PECORINO della
SABINA 14m.
€ 2,30 l'etto

PECORINO
CENERINO
€ 2,00 l'etto

PECORINO del
SABINA in
VINACCIA
€ 2,50 l'etto

about this book

OUR ROMAN RECIPES

The recipes in *Tasting Rome* include traditional dishes and contemporary innovations, each selected for the story it tells about Roman cuisine and the way it transports the full spectrum of local flavors to the home kitchen. Our recipes include and acknowledge classics like *Gricia* (see page 76) and *Coda alla Vaccinara* (page 147) and show how the cuisine has transitioned to include new dishes that draw on traditional flavors and ingredients. The classic dish *Cacio e Pepe* (page 74), a sauce of Pecorino Romano and coarsely ground black pepper, was once exclusively used as a condiment for pasta, but now has become a *Supplì* seasoning, too (see page 40). *Pollo alla Romana* (page 89), chicken simmered with tomaotes and bell peppers, used to be a main dish served on a platter during the summer; now you'll find it deboned and on sandwiches. The exciting thing about these innovations is that they are not radical, but instead deeply rooted in Roman flavors. They present the centuries-long evolution of the city's cuisine.

We have developed many of the classics for home use alongside the city's great chefs. We worked on the pizza and bread recipes with chef John Regefalk, an extraordinary baker and expert in European baking traditions, and many of the cocktails were created in collaboration with Rome's top mixologists, including Patrick Pistolesi and The Jerry Thomas Project.

It would be impossible to represent every aspect of the Roman dining experience, so we instead selected our recipes to highlight the *best* of Rome. Frankly, there are some really terrible classic and contemporary dishes being served today—and we have tried and suffered through them all so you don't have to. This book focuses on the foods that best communicate the spirit of the Roman flavors we have come to know and love.

Rather than dividing the book into traditional courses like *antipasto, primo, secondo, contorno,* and *dolce,* we chose an organization to accommodate the new classics and acknowledge noteworthy dishes. We included recipes without regard to critical mass in order to share the small but growing landscape of deliciously innovative Snacks, Starters, and Street Food. Our Classics draw on beloved recipes

perfected by hardworking local chefs, while the Variations are a nod to a new, lighter approach to cooking at home and in restaurants.

We pay special attention to two minority cuisines, Roman Jewish and Libyan Jewish, because a discussion of Roman food culture would be incomplete without recognizing the contributions of the *cucina ebraica romanesca* (page 105) and the more recent *cucina tripolina* (page 119). Although the Jewish community has just around 13,000 members, about .3 percent of the city's total population, the flavors and history of its dishes are so profoundly rich, they warrant special attention.

The Quinto Quarto chapter celebrates offal and poor cuts of meat, ingredients that have been used by peasants and nobles alike for millennia. We highlight some recipes that are slowly fading away and others that are becoming fashionable again, as young Roman chefs embrace flavors of the past. For all its meat and offal, Rome has profound affection for its seasonal produce, which floods market stalls and plays a supporting role in so many classic meals. Our Vegetable recipes revisit traditional dishes and propose new combinations, all of which celebrate local, seasonal items, and can be adapted to what is available to you.

The Bread and Pizza chapter is a survey of Roman-style baking and covers the popular local baked goods, from pizza and flatbreads to the sandwich rolls that anchor the everyday diet. We also pay tribute to ancient bakers and their heirloom wheats with an original loaf inspired by historical flavors. The Sweets chapter explores the underappreciated variety of Roman desserts, both baked and frozen. We chose our recipes to reflect holiday specialties and perennial favorites, plus a few inspired sweets, like *Sorbetto di Pesche e Vino* (page 208), that transform familiar flavors into new forms.

While cocktail culture is only just beginning to blossom, this movement has gained momentum as young Romans drift away from wine toward new flavors. Our recipes, adapted from bars or contributed by mixologists, are an insight into what they are thirsty for.

THE ROMAN KITCHEN

Eating in Rome can be intimidating—language barriers and separate menus for locals and tourists don't help—but cooking like a Roman shouldn't be. We recommend a few basic tools and ingredients to get you started so reproducing our recipes is a breeze, no matter how far from Rome you may be.

equipment

The Roman arsenal of tools is basic and practical, much like the cuisine itself, so you'll be able to cook Roman-style with even the simplest, no-frills equipment. Odds are, you already have the tools in your own kitchen. A handful of recipes call for special equipment—a pasta machine for *I Cracker* (page 190), for example—but most can be adapted to items you already have. If you have an ice cream maker or food processor, you're in good shape for making some of our frozen sweets. There's no need to run out and buy a pizza stone if you don't already have one; wherever possible we provide alternatives for special equipment. But here are a few things you *do* need.

BAKING DISHES AND BAKING PANS Baking dishes and pans come in various shapes, sizes, and materials (ceramic, porcelain, stoneware, Pyrex, and CorningWare, for example). If you don't have the size recommended in the recipe, you can use a smaller or larger vessel, but be aware that this may affect cooking time and adjust accordingly. The materials we suggest are the most reliable for even heating, but you can use any you already have.

For making bread, pizza, and pastries, weighing ingredients, even liquids, is a crucial step to success. Baking, after all, is an exact science. Cup measures can vary significantly and different flours have slightly differing weights per cup, so using a digital scale is the only foolproof method for ensuring you'll achieve the intended results. We highly recommend using metric measurements, and a digital kitchen scale that can switch between imperial and metric units is a handy tool for any kitchen. Metric measurements are more precise, and you'll notice that we have put them in parentheses beside the US measurements for bread and pizza recipes in the baking section. Please use them!

You'll need small, medium, and large bowls, preferably glass, stainless steel, or plastic, for mixing doughs, *Biga* (page 196), and porridge.

For the best results with pizza and bread, we highly recommend investing in a pizza stone, as well as a peel. Inverted baking sheets or unglazed quarry tiles make good substitutes. In all cases, you'll want to preheat the stone, baking sheet, or tile in the oven for at least 45 minutes before you bake. Doing so ensures that you will transfer the dough to the ideal surface for cooking it evenly. You can improvise a pizza peel with a flat, thin wooden board or a rimless baking sheet (see page 182). You'll need parchment paper to line baking sheets and to transfer the dough to the oven and onto your preferred preheated surface.

A dough scraper (also known as a bench scraper) can also be useful when handling and transferring dough. Think of it as a nonstick extension of your own hands. It also works wonders for cleaning your work surface, for dividing dough into segments, and for incising a loaf before baking it, as in the case of *Habemus Panem* (page 198); alternatively, you can use a chef's knife.

Baking sheets come in different sizes, the most versatile being a half sheet (18 × 13 inches). Our recipes were developed and tested using heavy gauge half-sheets, but in most cases, any size should work fine. Always line baking sheets with parchment paper or a nonstick silicone baking mat to prevent sticking.

BOX GRATER We recommend using a sturdy box grater with a good handle with at least one side of very small "punched" (protruding) holes. Use that side for grating Pecorino Romano and Parmigiano-

Reggiano to achieve a fine and powdery grate. Very fine, freshly grated cheese melts faster and more evenly and is less likely to clump, crucial for the most classic dishes like *Cacio e Pepe* (page 74), *Carbonara* (see page 70), and *Gricia* (see page 76).

COCKTAIL TOOLS Several of our cocktail recipes require a metal shaker, necessary for creating nice, frothy egg whites. Most basic shaker sets come with a Hawthorne strainer; use the strainer's detachable spring for dry shaking the *Cinquième Arrondissement* (page 233). You'll need large ice cube trays for the *Cosa Nostra* (page 234) and *Nerone* (page 237), which you can find at some liquor stores and online (see Resources, page 249). If you don't have a bar spoon, use a teaspoon, and if you have a jigger, use it for measuring spirits, or buy a set of small graduated liquid measures from OXO, which will be useful for most recipes in the book. BarProducts.com and Cocktail Kingdom are well stocked online outlets for cocktail tools in a range of prices (see Resources, page 249). Small, medium, and large jars will come in handy for *Sciroppo di Zucchero* (page 233), *Vodka all'Alloro* (page 237), *Digestivo all'Alloro* (page 239), and *Ciliegie al Mezcal* (page 242).

Our recipes suggest specific glassware for each drink, but if you don't have it, you don't have to run out and buy it. Our favorite bartenders change up their glassware all the time; we have been served the *Cinquième Arrondissement* in a wineglass, a Collins glass, and a pint glass. If Rome's bartenders are loose about how they serve drinks, you definitely can be, too.

FRYING IMPLEMENTS You certainly don't need a dedicated deep fryer to make the fried recipes—the small dimensions of Roman kitchens aren't amenable to appliances, so most home cooks just use a deep skillet, cast-iron pan, or Dutch oven. Use long tongs, a slotted deep-fry spoon, a long-handled mesh skimmer, or a metal frying basket to keep your distance from the hot oil. Manage oil temperatures with a sturdy thermometer with a temperature range up to 400°F. For deep-frying, we recommend using a vessel at least 6 inches deep. Higher sides reduce the risk of spillage or splashing. A wider pan is more stable, and therefore safer, than a narrow one, and the heavier the material, the more efficiently the pan maintains a consistent temperature, and therefore produces more consistent results. A double or triple timer helps manage timing when frying in batches.

ICE CREAM TOOLS You don't necessarily need an ice cream machine for making zabaione gelato for the *Affogato al Caffè* (page 204) or *Sorbetto di Pesche e Vino* (page 208); we offer an alternative method for freezing on page 204. But if you're in the market, the Cuisinart ICE-21 is a good entry-level model, while the De'Longhi GM6000 is a splurge. A small ice cream scoop (#60 scoop, which is the equivalent of 1 tablespoon) is useful for shaping and dropping *Castagnole* (page 207) and *Pizzarelle* (page 124), not to mention for serving gelato and sorbet.

POTS, PANS, AND SKILLETS In general, thicker-material pots, pans, and skillets heat more evenly and produce better results by maintaining a stable temperature while cooking. They are also less susceptible to large temperature fluctuations. Vessels made from thinner materials tend to distribute heat less evenly, leading to "hot spots" where food sticks and scorches.

For finishing pasta dishes in their sauce, we recommend using a stainless-steel pan at least 2 to 3 inches deep. The extra height makes it easier to toss and swirl the pasta as it cooks. A heavy-duty sauté pan with medium-high straight sides and a tight-fitting lid are ideal for braising meats. The pan size should allow the ingredients to fit snugly and cook together closely.

MIXERS Most stand mixers come with whisk, paddle, and dough hook attachments. The last is a great tool for kneading less hydrated and tougher dough and for long-duration mixing. You'll need a mixer with a dough hook for making *Pizza Romana* (page 181) and *Maritozzi con la Panna* (page 216). For the *Torta di Ricotta* (page 221) and the *Brutti ma Buoni* (page 224), if you don't have a stand mixer, you can use a hand mixer. Having an extra mixing bowl is always handy.

RAMEKINS Ramekins are small baking dishes made of porcelain or earthenware. We use 6-ounce ramekins for the *Sformatino di Broccolo Romanesco* (page 150) and 5½-ounce ramekins for the *Panna Cotta alla Menta con Salsa di Cioccolato* (page 212). In a pinch, ceramic cups, muffin tins, or even small jars could work as substitutes—and add character to your dining table.

ingredients

One of the most magical things about Rome is the abundance of seasonal produce sold in market stalls all over town. The flavor and intensity of these local ingredients are hard to match, but that doesn't mean you can't create food in the spirit of Rome in your own kitchen. Look for ingredients that at are the peak of freshness and flavor. Farmers' markets and community supported agriculture (CSA) organizations are a good place to start. If you're lucky enough to have a garden, you can even grow your own. Choosing your ingredients based on freshness and market availability is a way to add your own local flair to our recipes; this approach to shopping perfectly mirrors the spirit of Roman cooking.

Aside from produce, there are other items that will be an essential part of your Roman-style repertoire. We wrote this book with the home cook in mind, so you shouldn't have to search far and wide for supplies, but we have included some online resources for specialty items (see Resources, page 249).

BLACK PEPPER Considering how prevalent black pepper is in Roman cuisine today, it's hard to imagine that before the twentieth century it was a luxury for most. Perhaps to make up for lost time, Roman cooks use it liberally. When a recipe calls for black pepper, always use whole peppercorns and coarsely grind them fresh for each use.

EGGS Our recipes call for large eggs. Yolk color varies greatly; farm-raised organic eggs in Rome tend to have darker, more vibrant-colored yolks than their US (and even European) counterparts. This will impact the color, but not the flavor, of your *carbonara* (see page 70). If you are comfortable using raw egg whites for cocktails, be sure to use a fresh organic egg or get them from a trusted source; pasteurized egg whites or powdered egg whites work, too, and some say even better.

FENNEL POLLEN Seasoning pork with fennel pollen greatly complements its flavor and will enhance the flavors in the *Porchetta di Vito Bernabei* (page 103) beautifully. We also use it in *Habemus Panem* (page 198). It is available at specialty spice shops and via mail order (see Resources, page 249).

GUANCIALE *Guanciale* (page 82), a fatty, salt-cured pork jowl, is a cornerstone of Rome's pasta tradition. If you don't want to make it yourself, it is available at some Italian butchers and delis and via mail order (see Resources, page 249). Take care to slice off the outer layer of spice rub and any yellowed fat before dicing and cooking it. Cut it first into slabs like bacon so the pink and white parts run horizontally, then dice in the dimensions indicated in the recipe.

You can substitute *guanciale* with pancetta or slab bacon (both cured pork belly), which is used more or less interchangeably by Roman cooks, though bear in mind that *guanciale* is quite a bit fattier than pancetta (only about 30 percent lean compared to pancetta's 50 percent), so it will render more fat. If that scares you, feel free to remove some of the rendered fat from the pan. That tip may sound controversial, but we have seen plenty of Roman chefs do it while observing them in their kitchens. Some may disagree with removing *guanciale* fat from the pan, but others embrace it because it gives a lighter finished product. Don't discard it, though; you can use your rendered fat to make *Vodka al Guanciale* for *Carbonara Sour di Co.So.* (page 228).

OIL Unless otherwise noted, always use extra-virgin olive oil, whether for cooking vegetables or for dressing a salad. For frying, use neutral oil with a high smoking point: rapeseed, canola, peanut, or corn.

PASTA We recommend using the highest-quality pasta you can afford. Slow-dried, bronze-extruded, durum wheat pasta has excellent structure and flavor and will improve the quality of a dish. Pastificio Di Martino and Whole Foods 365 brands are good mid-range options. Benedetto Cavalieri, Pastificio dei Campi, Felicetti, and Setaro are high-end brands, and worth it.

In each dish, we specify a pasta shape. Thanks to food historians Oretta Zanini De Vita and Maureen Fant, there is an entire book (*Sauces & Shapes: Pasta the Italian Way*) devoted to the theory behind pairing sauces with specific pasta shapes, and the proper pairing really *does* matter to Romans—and to most Italians, for that matter. The classic Roman pasta arsenal includes spaghetti, rigatoni, and *bombolotti* (also called *mezze maniche*).

PECORINO ROMANO Pecorino Romano is a salted sheep's-milk cheese that has roots in Rome stretching back two thousand years. In spite of the name, it's not necessarily produced in Rome; by law, it can be made in Sardinia and southern Tuscany as well. Each producer has his or her own approach to *salatura* (salting), so the saltiness of the cheese may differ from brand to brand, and the same producer's cheese will vary throughout the season. Taste cheese before using it in a recipe and be conservative when adding salt to dishes that feature it. In Rome, we use Brunelli and Lopez brands. Specialty Italian shops and cheese mongers in the United States (see page 249) stock mid- and high-range cheeses. Trader Joe's is a respectable and affordable supermarket brand, and Whole Foods and Bristol Farms also have a selection, though at a higher price range.

PEPERONCINO When it comes to spices, the Roman palate doesn't crave intense or prolonged heat, but *peperoncino*, a mild to moderate strength chile, is a staple. We use dried *peperoncino* here—market stalls sell it from hanging strands—but you can use dried chile flakes or fresh Thai bird's-eye chiles for a similar effect.

SALT Always use sea salt unless otherwise noted, like for salting meats and fish when kosher salt is used instead. Salt meats well in advance to allow the seasoning to penetrate the meat; salt whole fish just an hour before cooking. For fillets, salt 20 minutes before cooking.

OLd'sC

VERMOUTH · Dri

the

SPIRITS

chiedere

VINi · BIT

how to use this book

Our recipes are divided by theme, and you can jump around and
mix and match dishes based on the season, the holiday, or what your
appetite craves. There are a few things to note before you dive in,
though.

measurements and seasoning

We wrote these recipes in the spirit of Roman cooking, which doesn't
get bogged down with precise ingredient amounts or proportions,
except when baking bread and pizza or curing *Guanciale* (page 82).
Flip through any Italian cookbook for proof—you are guaranteed to see
the abbreviation "q.b." peppered throughout its pages. *Quanto basta*,
"as much as you need," indicates a personal preference to ingredient
amounts and proportions, so know that our recipes are guidelines that
may be adjusted to your personal palate.

    While Roman recipes might indicate "a handful" or "a glass
of" without defining precise quantities, we have written the recipes
using US measurements. We very strongly urge you to use the metric
measurements listed in parentheses for bread and pizza baking recipes
to achieve the most successful and precise results.

    Always read the entire recipe before beginning to cook. Some
recipes require prep work in advance, which will be mentioned in the
headnote. We almost always recommend salting proteins before cooking
them. Salting meat and fish in advance gives the salt time to penetrate
and flavor the meat. Tough cuts and whole muscles benefit from salting
a day ahead, while smaller cuts and fish can be seasoned for a shorter
length of time.

    When salting water for cooking pasta or vegetables, use enough salt
to achieve the saltiness of seawater.

    As we mentioned, Pecorino Romano is already salted; taste the
cheese before adding extra salt so you don't overdo it. You'll see that we
don't add any salt to the *Supplì Cacio e Pepe* (page 40) and we salt the
water sparingly when making *Cacio e Pepe* (page 74).

pasta and rice

Most of our pasta dishes yield four to six servings per pound of pasta. Traditionally, Romans eat in courses: a *primo* (usually pasta or soup) followed by a *secondo* (meat or fish). If you plan to do the same, the pasta course should feed six. If you are treating it as your main dish, the recipe serves four.

Cook the pasta to the recommended doneness. Al dente means the pasta still has some firmness and bite to it. Taste the pasta as it cooks and cook until it is still firm and most of the white part in the middle is cooked through. Rice is al dente when it still has a tiny bit of white in the center but it isn't chalky. The *Bombolotti all'Amatriciana* (page 77), *Amatriciana Estiva* (page 79), *Spaghetti alla Gricia di Claudio Gargioli* (page 76), and *Pomodori con Riso* (page 159) call for "very al dente" pasta or rice. Romans call this cooking approach *al chiodo*, "like an iron nail." In those cases, the pasta and rice should both still be partially raw so you can finish cooking in a secondary step. The pastas in both *Amatriciana* recipes finish cooking in their sauces with lots of pasta water added. The pasta absorbs the liquid as it cooks. When it is al dente after that step, it's done.

baking

Our bread and pizza dough should be worked by hand, unless otherwise noted. Learn the basic methods we recommend and feel free to make small changes in your cooking as necessary to accommodate any differences in flour—all flours are different, so they absorb water at different rates.

Higher temperatures cause dough to rise faster at the cost of flavor, while lower temperatures contribute to a slower rise and more complex flavors—that's why we suggest cold fermenting some of the dough in the refrigerator before baking. When we say room temperature, we always mean on the warmer side, around 71°F to 77°F. With a bit of tweaking to adapt to your environment, you should be able to reproduce our dough just about anywhere.

We'll refer back to these pages throughout the recipes so you can access them easily as you cook. With all of this, what you already have in your kitchen, and your curiosity or love for this ancient city, you're ready to start *Tasting Rome*!

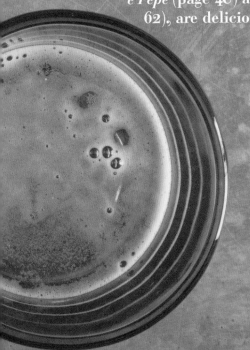

SNACKS, STARTERS, AND STREET FOOD

Roman snacks are meant to feel light and digestible, even when deep-fried (which is often). Portions are small and usually portable when served at takeaway shops, while starters served at home or restaurant tables should whet the appetite and pave the way for the multicourse meal that follows. Some of our snacks are strictly traditional, like *Supplì Classici* (page 38) or *Fave, Pecorino, e Corallina* (page 56), while others, like *Supplì Cacio e Pepe* (page 40) and *Crostini con Burro e Alici* (page 62), are delicious twists on a celebrated form.

supplì classici

CLASSIC RICE CROQUETTES

RISOTTO and other rice dishes are common in many parts of Italy, but rice doesn't play a huge role in Roman cuisine. This fact helps make a case for *supplì*, rice croquettes, as an import. Some say their name comes from the French word *surprise* and credits Napoleon's troops for bringing them over in the early nineteenth century. Whatever their origin, *supplì* are served at Rome's pizzerias and pizza by the slice shops, though most are mass-produced frozen versions with a scary fluorescent orange crust and a filling of meat sauce and mozzarella. The old-school homemade variety used chicken innards instead of beef, and often bits of sausage as well. This classic version reaches its apex at Supplizio and L'Arcangelo, two venues owned by chef Arcangelo Dandini, Rome's undisputed *supplì* (and gnocchi!) master. A crispy exterior gives way to a rich mixture of rice, chicken livers, and pork sausage in a tomato-based sauce. The "surprise" is a bit of melted mozzarella in the center. Our recipe and Arcangelo's are based on Ada Boni's version, from her iconic cookbook *The Talisman Italian Cookbook.*

makes 10 **supplì**

2 tablespoons extra-virgin olive oil

3 ounces pork sausage, casings removed

½ yellow onion, finely chopped (about ⅓ cup)

3 ounces chicken livers, finely chopped

1 cup (7 ounces) Arborio rice

½ cup white wine

2 cups beef broth, warmed

1 cup (8 ounces) tomato sauce, warmed

3 to 4 fresh basil leaves (optional)

⅔ cup grated Pecorino Romano

Line a large platter or baking sheet with parchment paper.

Heat the olive oil in a medium skillet over medium heat. When the oil begins to shimmer, add the sausage in small pieces and cook, breaking up the meat with a spoon as it cooks, until lightly browned, about 3 minutes. Add the onion and cook until softened and translucent, about 10 minutes. Add the chicken livers and stir, breaking them up with a wooden spoon, until cooked, about 5 minutes. Add the rice and stir to coat. Continue stirring until the rice is lightly toasted and becomes translucent, about 2 minutes, then add the wine. Stir until the alcohol aroma dissipates, about 1 minute, then add 1 cup of the broth. Cook, stirring continuously to prevent the rice from sticking to the pan, until the broth has been absorbed, about 3 minutes. Add the tomato sauce and cook, stirring continuously, until it has been absorbed, 5 minutes more. Add another ½ cup broth, stirring continously, until it has been absorbed, 8 to 10 minutes. If, once the rice has absorbed the broth, more liquid is needed, add the remaining ½ cup broth. The rice is done when it is al dente (see page 34).

1 tablespoon unsalted butter

Sea salt and freshly ground black pepper

1 cup all-purpose flour

2 large eggs

1 cup bread crumbs

3 ounces mozzarella, cut into 10 equal pieces

Neutral oil (see page 27), for frying

Keep the beef broth simmering on the stove so that when you add it to the rice, it doesn't stop the cooking. For the same reason, use tomato sauce that is warmed on the stove.

Remove the pan from the heat and stir in the basil (if using), Pecorino Romano, and butter. Season to taste. Spread the rice over the prepared baking sheet and refrigerate until cool, about 1 hour.

Meanwhile, set up your breading station: Place the flour on a plate or in a shallow bowl. Beat the eggs in a medium bowl. Place the bread crumbs on a plate or in a shallow bowl. Season the flour, eggs, and bread crumbs with salt.

Remove the baking sheet from the refrigerator and form the rice into ten equal-size, egg-shaped balls. Working with one at a time, hold the ball in your palm and make a depression in the center. Place a piece of mozzarella in the depression and re-form the rice around the mozzarella. If the balls aren't holding together, return them to the refrigerator for 30 minutes more after shaping.

Dredge each *supplì* first in flour, shaking off excess, then dip in egg, allowing excess to drip off, and finally coat in bread crumbs. Repeat for a thicker crust, if desired. Set aside.

In a medium frying pan or cast-iron skillet, heat 2 inches of neutral oil to 350°F. Fry the *supplì* in batches, until deep golden brown, 3 to 4 minutes, turning once to ensure even browning.

Drain on paper towels, sprinkle with salt, and serve hot.

supplì cacio e pepe

RICE CROQUETTES WITH PECORINO ROMANO AND BLACK PEPPER

ROME'S *Supplì Classici* (page 38) were the standard for about a century, but recently they have been joined by a handful of creative variations. The city's top pizzerias, such as Sforno, Tonda, and Pizzarium, were the first places to experiment with seasonings that break with tradition, paving the way for an even wider range of rice croquettes. Some places even substitute pasta for rice! This variation riffs on *Cacio e Pepe* (page 74), the classic Roman pasta. The results are a peppery snack rooted in the modern flavors of Rome. In fact, black pepper, which is such an essential part of the *cucina romana* today, only entered the mainstream in the twentieth century. Before that, it was an expensive luxury.

makes 10 **supplì**

2 tablespoons extra-virgin olive oil

½ yellow onion, finely chopped (about ⅓ cup)

1 cup (7 ounces) Arborio rice

½ cup white wine

3 cups chicken or vegetable broth, warmed

¾ cup grated Pecorino Romano

1 teaspoon freshly ground black pepper, plus more to taste

1 tablespoon unsalted butter

Sea salt

1 cup all-purpose flour

2 large eggs

1 cup bread crumbs

3 ounces mozzarella, cut into 10 equal pieces

Neutral oil (see page 27), for frying

Line a large platter or baking sheet with parchment paper.

Heat the olive oil in a medium skillet over medium heat. When the oil begins to shimmer, add the onion and cook until softened and translucent, about 10 minutes. Add the rice and stir to coat. Continue stirring until the rice is lightly toasted and becomes translucent, about 2 minutes, then add the wine. Stir until the alcohol aroma dissipates, about 1 minute, then add 1 cup of the broth. Cook, stirring continuously to prevent the rice from sticking to the pan, until the broth has been absorbed, about 3 minutes. Add another cup of the broth and cook, stirring continuously, until it has been absorbed, about 5 minutes more. If necessary, add more liquid ¼ cup at a time, stirring until it has been absorbed and testing for doneness. (You may not need all the broth.) The rice is done when it is al dente (see page 34).

Remove the pan from the heat, stir in the Pecorino Romano, pepper, and butter, and mix well. Season to taste. Spread the rice over the prepared baking sheet and refrigerate until cool, about 1 hour.

Meanwhile, set up your breading station: Place the flour on a plate or in a shallow bowl. Beat the eggs in a medium bowl. Place the bread crumbs on a plate or in a shallow bowl.

Don't season the bread crumbs this time. Pecorino Romano and any seasoning added to taste brings enough flavor to the dish on their own!

Remove the baking sheet from the refrigerator and form the rice into ten equal-size, egg-shaped balls. Working with one at a time, hold the ball in your palm and make a depression in the center. Place a piece of mozzarella in the depression and re-form the rice around the mozzarella. If the balls aren't holding together, return them to the refrigerator for 30 minutes more after shaping.

Dredge each *supplì* first in flour, shaking off excess, then dip in egg, allowing excess to drip off, and finally coat in bread crumbs. Repeat for a thicker crust, if desired. Set aside.

In a medium frying pan or cast-iron skillet, heat 2 inches of neutral oil to 350°F. Fry the *supplì* in batches, until deep golden brown, 3 to 4 minutes, turning once to ensure even browning.

Drain on paper towels, and serve hot.

supplì radicchio e gorgonzola

RICE CROQUETTES WITH RADICCHIO AND GORGONZOLA

BITTER RADICCHIO and pungent Gorgonzola are northern Italian ingredients that have made their way down the peninsula and are often paired together on pizzas or even in pasta dishes in Rome. This *supplì* variation plays on the beautiful flavor and color contrasts that come from that combination. The rice mingles with the creamy cheese, sweet onion, and bitter radicchio for a purple-tinged twist on *Supplì Classici* (page 38).

makes 10 supplì

2 tablespoons extra-virgin olive oil	Line a large platter or baking sheet with parchment paper.
½ yellow onion, finely chopped (about ⅓ cup)	Heat the olive oil in a medium skillet over medium heat. When the oil begins to shimmer, add the onion and cook until softened and translucent, about 10 minutes. Add the rice and stir to coat. Continue stirring until the rice is lightly toasted and becomes translucent, about 2 minutes, then add the wine. Stir until the alcohol aroma dissipates, about 1 minute, then add 1 cup of the broth. Cook, stirring continuously to prevent the rice from sticking to the pan, until the broth has been absorbed, about 3 minutes. Add the radicchio and another cup of the broth and cook, stirring continuously, until it has been absorbed, about 5 minutes more. If necessary, add more liquid ¼ cup at a time, stirring until it has been absorbed and testing for doneness. (You may not need all the broth.) The rice is done when it is al dente (see page 34).
1 cup (7 ounces) Arborio rice	
½ cup red wine	
3 cups chicken or vegetable broth, warmed	
3½ cups finely chopped radicchio	
3½ ounces Gorgonzola, cut into small pieces	
3 tablespoons grated Parmigiano-Reggiano	Remove the pan from the heat, stir in the Gorgonzola, Parmigiano-Reggiano, pepper, and butter, and mix well. Season to taste. Spread the rice over the prepared baking sheet and refrigerate until cool, about 1 hour.
Freshly ground black pepper	
1 tablespoon unsalted butter	
Sea salt	Meanwhile, set up your breading station: Place the flour on a plate or in a shallow bowl. Beat the eggs in a medium bowl. Place the bread crumbs on a plate or in a shallow bowl. Season the flour, eggs, and bread crumbs with salt.
1 cup all-purpose flour	
2 large eggs	
1 cup bread crumbs	
3 ounces mozzarella, cut into 10 equal pieces	Remove the baking sheet from the refrigerator and form the rice into ten equal-size, egg-shaped balls. Working with one at a time, hold the ball in your palm and make a depression in the center. Place a piece of mozzarella in the depression and re-form the rice around the mozzarella. If the balls aren't
Neutral oil (see page 27), for frying	

holding together, return them to the refrigerator for 30 minutes more after shaping.

Dredge each *supplì* first in flour, shaking off excess, then dip in egg, allowing excess to drip off, and finally coat in bread crumbs. Repeat for a thicker crust, if desired. Set aside.

In a medium frying pan or cast-iron skillet, heat 2 inches of neutral oil to 350°F. Fry the *supplì* in batches, until deep golden brown, 3 to 4 minutes, turning once to ensure even browning.

Drain on paper towels, sprinkle with salt, and serve hot.

cazzimperio

CRUDITÉS

CAZZIMPERIO (also known as *pinzimonio,* or crudités) pretty much sums up Rome's relationship with raw vegetables. Elsewhere, you might be served carrot sticks or celery stalks with a thick, creamy dipping sauce. Not in Rome. Here, the only accompaniment is a good, green olive oil from nearby groves. *Cazzimperio* is best enjoyed with extra-virgin olive oil from the Sabina, an area in northern Lazio known for its sensational oils, but you can substitute any good-quality unfiltered extra-virgin olive oil with rich flavor and a clean finish.

serves 4 to 6

¼ cup extra-virgin olive oil

¼ teaspoon sea salt

¼ teaspoon freshly ground black pepper

3 carrots, quartered lengthwise and cut into 4-inch sticks

3 celery stalks, sliced in half lengthwise and cut into 4-inch sticks

1 romaine lettuce heart, leaves separated

2 fennel bulbs, thickly sliced

12 radishes

In a small bowl, combine the olive oil, salt, and pepper.

Arrange the raw vegetables on a serving platter. Serve with the seasoned olive oil alongside.

torta rustica

SAVORY PIE

TORTE RUSTICHE feature prominently on Rome's wine bar menus and in local bakeries. Fillings may change with the seasons; the vegetal ingredients in this recipe, carrots included, grow in the Roman countryside. In Rome, you're most likely to find this savory delight served as a snack alongside Prosecco or a cold beer when you're dining al fresco, but you can also serve it as a starter, or even as a light main dish. The flaky crust can either be a quick dough called rough puff pastry, or you can use store-bought.

makes 1 torta rustica, *to serve 6 to 8*

1 teaspoon sea salt, plus more for salting the water

1 pound fresh spinach leaves

1 pound fresh chard

¼ pound dandelion greens

2 tablespoons extra-virgin olive oil

1 onion, coarsely chopped

3 tablespoons chopped fresh flat-leaf parsley

½ carrot, finely grated

½ pound ricotta

1¼ cups grated Parmigiano-Reggiano

4 large eggs

Freshly ground black pepper

1 pound rough puff pastry, homemade (page 186) or store-bought

Bring a large pot of water to a boil over high heat. Salt the water. When the salt has dissolved, add the spinach, chard, and dandelion greens and blanch for 1 minute, until the stalks are tender. Drain and allow to cool, about 20 minutes. Squeeze out excess water very well and chop into small, confetti-size pieces.

Heat the olive oil in a large skillet over medium heat. When the oil begins to shimmer, add the onion and cook until softened and translucent, about 10 minutes. Add the greens and cook until they are tender and have darkened, 15 minutes more.

Transfer the greens to a large bowl and add the parsley, carrot, salt, ricotta, Parmigiano-Reggiano, three of the eggs, and pepper to taste. Mix well and set aside.

Preheat the oven to 400°F. Line an 8-inch pie pan with parchment paper.

In a small bowl, lightly beat the remaining egg. Set aside.

Slice off a third of the puff pastry and set aside. On a lightly floured surface, roll the remaining pastry into a 10-inch round, ⅛ inch thick. Place the pastry in the prepared pan, pressing it into the corners and leaving enough overhang to rest on the top edge of the pie pan. Trim the excess pastry with a knife. Spoon the filling into the pastry and level it to the top of the pie pan.

RECIPE CONTINUES

Roll out the reserved pastry into a 10 × 6-inch rectangle. With a knife or fluted pastry wheel, cut it into twelve ½-inch-wide strips. Use these to make a lattice over the top of the pie, trimming the excess strips and pressing them to adhere to the edge of the bottom layer of pastry. Brush the lattice with the beaten egg.

Bake for 40 to 45 minutes, or until the crust is golden brown.

Remove the *torta rustica* from the oven and allow it to rest for at least 30 minutes before serving. The pie is best served at room temperature. It will keep in the refrigerator, covered, for 2 days; remove it from the refrigerator 1 hour before serving.

To achieve a woven lattice: Arrange six strips of dough vertically over the filling, spacing them evenly apart. Gently fold back every other strip three-quarters of the way.

Beginning on the side where the strips are folded back, lay down a new strip of dough horizontally, closest to where the three strips are folded back. Unfold the folded strips so they cover the newly laid strip of dough, and fold back the three strips that were not previously folded. Lay another strip down horizontally, then unfold the folded strips on top of the newly laid strip.

Repeat with the remaining strips of dough to complete the woven effect.

Trim the strips even with the edge of the pie. Moisten the underside of each with water and press to adhere.

TRAPIZZINO

Stefano Callegari found the perfect balance between traditional flavors and new forms when he invented the *trapizzino* at his hole-in-the-wall pizza by the slice joint in 2009. To produce it, he bakes naturally leavened, fluffy triangles of *Pizza Bianca* (page 175), slices them open on one side, and fills them with the hearty classics of the *cucina romana*.

The word *trapizzino* is a clever mash-up of two popular snack names: *tramezzino* and pizza. Cafés everywhere serve triangular white bread sandwiches called *tramezzini*. These tricornered sandwiches are toasted on a panini press and served as a late-morning or afternoon snack. Pizza by the slice, on the other hand, is pizza baked in rectangular trays and sold by weight—it's the most Roman of fast foods. Romans have embraced Callegari's *trapizzino* because, aside from its undeniable deliciousness, it merges ideas already rooted in local culture. In other words, it's not a huge stretch for tradition-driven locals to latch onto a new item that draws on existing foods. It offers the flavors they crave, but in a convenient new package adapted to today's tough economic climate.

As a clever businessman keenly aware of Rome's obsession with its native flavors, Callegari selects fillings with cultural relevance, for example *Lingua in Salsa Verde* (page 139), *Pollo alla Romana* (page 89), and *Coda alla Vaccinara* (page 147), all of which are main courses in homes and restaurants. *Trapizzino* fillings are particularly offal heavy because the snack was invented in Testaccio (see page 132), a neighborhood known for the so-called *quinto quarto* ("fifth quarter"). Callegari doesn't limit his fillings to traditional Roman dishes, but also makes non-Roman items like *zighinì*, a spiced beef stew from East Africa, which acknowledges the city's long-established immigrant communities from Ethiopia, Eritrea, and Somalia. When viewed as a whole, his *trapizzino* menu perfectly encapsulates Rome's local flavors, both native and imported.

polpette di bollito

DEEP-FRIED SHREDDED BEEF MEATBALLS

THE WORD *polpette* (meatballs) is a term that encompasses a whole range of round-shaped snacks, meaty and otherwise. *Polpette di bollito* fall into the former category and are traditionally cooked from leftover meat as a way to make the most of it. The meat is shredded and shaped, then breaded and fried. This recipe is inspired by that of Cesare al Casaletto, a trattoria in the Gianicolense district of Rome that specializes in fried starters. To serve your *polpette* Cesare style, add a dollop of *Salsa Verde* (page 139). Alternatively, serve with a wedge of lemon—the acid will help cut through the fat. Salt the beef with kosher salt at least 4 hours, and up to 24 hours, in advance.

makes 20 **polpette**

1 pound beef shin or trim, connective tissue removed, salted in advance

1 cup dry white wine

3 carrots

2 yellow onions

10 whole black peppercorns

2 whole cloves

1 potato, peeled, boiled, and cubed

3½ ounces mortadella, sliced into strips

⅓ cup grated Parmigiano-Reggiano

2 tablespoons finely chopped fresh flat-leaf parsley

4 large eggs

Sea salt

1 cup all-purpose flour

1 cup fine bread crumbs

Neutral oil (see page 27), for frying

Place the salted beef in a large pot. Cover with cold water and bring to a simmer over medium heat, skimming off any foam that rises to the top. Then reduce the heat to low and add the wine, carrots, onions, peppercorns, and cloves. Keep at a low simmer until the beef is fork-tender, 1½ to 2 hours.

Transfer the beef to a plate or cutting board; strain and reserve the broth (discard the solids) for *Supplì Classici* (page 38), *Simmenthal di Coda* (page 144), or another dish. Using tongs or two forks, shred the beef into small pieces, then transfer to a food processor. Add the potato and mortadella and pulse to break them up. If the mixture looks dry, add reserved broth 1 tablespoon at a time to moisten. The mixture should be in small pieces, and nearly a paste. Transfer to a medium bowl and add the Parmigiano-Reggiano, parsley, and two of the eggs. Mix well with your hands or a wooden spoon. Season to taste and refrigerate for about an hour so the mixture is easier to work with.

Meanwhile, set up your breading station: Place the flour on a plate or in a shallow bowl. Beat the remaining two eggs in a medium bowl. Place the bread crumbs on a plate or in a shallow bowl. Season the flour, eggs, and bread crumbs with salt. Set aside.

Remove the beef mixture from the refrigerator and form it into twenty equal-size meatballs, about the size of walnuts. Dredge

each one first in flour, shaking off excess, then dip in egg, allowing excess to drip off, and finally coat in bread crumbs. Repeat for a thicker crust, if desired. Set aside.

In a medium frying pan or cast-iron skillet, heat 2 inches of neutral oil to 350°F. Fry the meatballs in batches, taking care not to overcrowd the pan, until a nice golden brown crust has formed, 3 to 4 minutes, turning once to ensure even browning.

Drain on paper towels, sprinkle with salt, and serve hot.

Use semi-dry mozzarella, if possible. If the cheese is very wet and liquidy, set it on a wire rack, cover the cheese with parchment paper, place a weight on top (a cast-iron skillet works well), and drain for an hour or two. You can use buffalo mozzarella instead of cow's-milk mozzarella here.

'nduja in carrozza

FRIED MOZZARELLA WITH 'NDUJA

TRADITIONAL *mozzarella in carrozza* features slices of mozzarella sandwiched between slices of bread, which is then battered and panfried. It's a child's snack that is equally comforting to adults; it's mainly reserved for the home table—think Rome's answer to grilled cheese. Gabriele Bonci, a legendary baker and owner of Rome's landmark pizza by the slice joint Pizzarium, is constantly tweaking traditional foods and forms. His so-called *'nduja in carrozza* is a prime example of his approach to cooking. Bonci's twist omits the bread altogether. Instead, slices of mozzarella are filled with a smear of 'nduja, a spreadable, spicy salami from Calabria, then breaded and deep-fried. When split open, the red-hot chile oil and melted mozzarella mix with each savory bite. If a southern Italian salami seems out of place in Rome, consider that around four hundred thousand of its residents have Calabrian roots. 'Nduja is becoming more readily available in the United States, but if you can't get your hands on some, substitute another spicy pork product like thin slices of hot capicola or finely chopped bits of *soppressata*.

makes 6 'nduja in carrozza

---

12 ounces mozzarella, cut into 12 slices

2 tablespoons 'nduja

1 cup all-purpose flour

2 large eggs

1 cup bread crumbs

Sea salt and freshly ground black pepper

Neutral oil (see page 27), for frying

Pat the mozzarella slices dry. Spread 1 teaspoon of the 'nduja on one side of each of six slices, then top with the remaining slices to form six "sandwiches." Set aside.

Set up your breading station: Place the flour on a plate or in a shallow bowl. Beat the eggs in a medium bowl. Place the bread crumbs on a plate or in a shallow bowl. Season the flour, eggs, and bread crumbs with salt and pepper.

Dredge each "sandwich" first in flour, shaking off excess, then in egg, allowing excess to drip off, and finally coat in bread crumbs. Repeat for a thicker crust, if desired, to prevent the cheese from leaking out during frying. Set aside.

In a medium frying pan or cast-iron skillet, heat 2 inches of neutral oil to 350°F. Fry the "sandwiches" in batches, until deep golden brown, 3 to 4 minutes, turning once to ensure even browning.

Drain on paper towels, sprinkle with salt, and serve hot.

fave, pecorino, e corallina

FAVA BEANS, PECORINO, AND SALAMI

IN ITALY, May 1 is Labor Day, a national holiday dedicated to workers. In Rome, it's a time to either go to the concerts and left-wing gatherings in front of San Giovanni in Laterano, Rome's cathedral, or visit the countryside for a long picnic beneath shady umbrella pines. Either way, every holiday feast starts with a heap of fresh fava bean pods and wedges of Pecorino Romano, sharp and salty sheep's-milk cheese. This classic Roman combo transcends political affiliations. We like to throw a bit of *corallina* into the mix, too, as the peppery local salami studded with big cubes of fat is another classic springtime element on Roman tables. Serve the seasonal trio on a cutting board or simple platter and, of course, eat it with your hands. Serve with a slightly chilled red wine, ideally made from local grapes like Cesanese, Nero Buono, or Montepulciano.

serves 4 to 6

8 to 10 ounces Pecorino Romano

8 to 10 ounces *corallina* salami or other coarse pork salami with black pepper

1½ pounds fresh fava beans in pods

Using a knife, split the Pecorino Romano into bite-size chunks along the natural grain of the cheese (do not slice it). Slice the salami crosswise into ⅛-inch-thick rounds, removing and discarding the outer casing. Arrange the cheese and salami on a cutting board or platter. Pile the fava bean pods alongside.

Serve picnic style.

filetti di baccalà

FRIED COD FILLETS

A PRODUCT of northern Europe, *baccalà*, dried and salted cod, has long been a staple of Rome's cuisine. Even though Rome is close to the Tyrrhenian Sea, the city once depended on distant sources for its fish supply. *Baccalà* appears in a variety of dishes, from soups to stews, and was a common feature on tables of all faiths. The battered and deep-fried version, called *filetti di baccalà*, originated in the Jewish Ghetto, where street food stalls catered to an impoverished public. Today, this dish appears on pizzeria and restaurant menus and is sparsely seasoned with just salt and lemon—it's like Rome's version of fish and chips, just minus the chips.

makes 12 filetti di baccalà

1 cup all-purpose flour, plus ⅓ cup for dredging

1 large egg, separated

2 tablespoons white wine

⅛ teaspoon sea salt, plus more to taste

1 pound salt cod fillets, soaked, rinsed, and cut into 12 equal pieces

Neutral oil (see page 27), for frying

1 lemon, cut into wedges

To remove salt from the cod, soak in abundant water for at least 24 hours, changing the water at least four times, until the water (and therefore the fish) is no longer salty.

In a shallow medium bowl, combine 1 cup of the flour, the egg yolk, wine, salt, and 1 cup water and whisk until smooth. In a separate medium bowl, whip the egg white to firm peaks. Then gently fold it into the batter.

Pat the cod dry with paper towels, season with salt, then toss in the remaining ⅓ cup flour to coat, shaking off any excess. Set aside.

In a medium frying pan or cast-iron skillet, heat 2 inches of neutral oil to 350°F. Using a fork, dip the cod into the batter, allowing the excess to drip off, then carefully lower it into the oil. Fry the battered cod in batches, turning once to ensure even browning, until lightly browned, about 5 minutes.

Drain on paper towels, sprinkle with salt, and serve immediately with wedges of lemon.

fiori di zucca e pezzetti fritti

FRIED SQUASH BLOSSOMS AND SEASONAL FRUITS AND VEGETABLES

HOLIDAY TABLES are rarely without *pezzetti fritti*, fried starters served family style. When zucchini and squash are in season, the male flowers (*fiori di zucca*) are filled with mozzarella and anchovies, battered, and fried. Roman batter is thick and obscures whatever it encases; we propose a lighter batter, kept very cold to achieve a delicate outcome.

serves 4 to 6

FOR THE SQUASH BLOSSOMS

3 salted anchovies, cleaned (see page 116), filleted, and halved lengthwise and crosswise

4 ounces mozzarella, cut into 12 equal pieces

12 squash blossoms, cleaned, dried, stamen removed, and stem trimmed to about 1 inch

Neutral oil (see page 27), for frying

FOR THE BATTER

2 cups all-purpose flour

Pinch of sea salt

2⅔ cups sparkling ice water

FOR THE SEASONAL FRUITS AND VEGETABLES

2 apples, peeled, cored, and cut into ½-inch wedges

2 cups cauliflower florets

2 cups romanesco florets

4 tender young artichokes (any kind), cleaned and cut into ½-inch wedges (see page 167)

Make the squash blossoms: Place one piece of anchovy and one piece of mozzarella inside each squash blossom, taking care not to tear the petals. Set aside.

In a medium frying pan or cast-iron skillet, heat 2 inches of neutral oil to 350°F.

Make the batter: Fill a large bowl with ice water and rest a second medium bowl inside. Combine the flour, salt, and sparkling water in the medium bowl and whisk until smooth. To keep the batter as cold as possible between batches, replenish the ice in the large bowl below.

Working one at a time, hold the closed flower tips and dip the squash blossoms into the batter to coat thoroughly. Allow excess to drip off, taking care to ensure that the flower tips are battered shut. Lower the blossoms into the oil and fry in batches until lightly browned, 2 to 3 minutes, turning once to ensure even browning.

Drain on paper towels. Sprinkle with salt.

Batter and fry the apples, cauliflower, romanesco, and artichokes, dipping each piece individually into the batter, then frying in batches. Drain on paper towels and sprinkle with salt.

Serve *fiori di zucca* and *pezzetti fritti* immediately on a large platter.

When frying, the trick to making the end product feel and taste light is to regulate the temperature of the oil to ensure even cooking. The temperature naturally drops when battered items are added, especially if your pan is overcrowded. Use a frying thermometer to manage it.

olive marinate

MARINATED OLIVES

PEOPLE often ask us if there are restaurants in Rome that specialize in ancient Roman recipes. Not really. As fun as it is (for us, at least) to geek out on ancient cookbooks, not everything the Romans ate in antiquity translates well to the modern table—a dish of sterile sow's womb with black pepper and honey comes to mind. But our marinated olives, which *are* inspired by an ancient recipe (the orator Cato's, to be exact), embrace flavors that are just as relevant today as they were two thousand years ago.

makes 1 pound of olives

1 pound Gaeta olives

1 teaspoon coriander seeds

1 teaspoon cumin seeds

1 teaspoon fennel seeds

2 garlic cloves, unpeeled

1 sprig fresh rosemary

1 sprig fresh sage

1 bay leaf

1 tablespoon white wine vinegar

Pinch of *peperoncino* or red pepper flakes

2 cups extra-virgin olive oil

For best results, make these olives a day ahead, allowing them to sit in their cooking oil. The flavors will marry and intensify as the cooked olives marinate in the oil and spices.

Soak the olives in abundant water to remove excess salt, about 2 hours. They are ready when they no longer taste of salt.

Preheat the oven to 275°F.

Drain the olives and place them in a medium bowl. Toss with the coriander, cumin, fennel, garlic, rosemary, sage, bay leaf, vinegar, and *peperoncino*. Mix well to evenly distribute all the herbs and spices. Transfer to a small baking dish and add the olive oil. The olives should be almost completely submerged.

Cover with aluminum foil and bake for 2 hours, stirring occasionally.

Remove from the oven and allow the olives to cool completely, about 1 hour. Strain, reserving the cooking oil to dress a salad, or to drizzle on meat or pasta. Serve the olives at room temperature alongside your favorite *apéritif*.

crostini con burro e alici

BUTTER AND ANCHOVY CROSTINI

SALTY ANCHOVIES and rich, subtly sweet butter pair brilliantly together; the two tossed with spaghetti equal pure Roman comfort food. Transform this savory combo into a delectable snack by spreading a thick layer of butter over toast to serve alongside a glass of sparkling wine or a cocktail. We like to use a crusty local sourdough, *pane di Lariano*, but you can use any rustic loaf.

makes 6 crostini

2 tablespoons unsalted butter

6 thin slices sourdough bread, toasted

3 salted anchovies, cleaned (see page 116), filleted, and halved lengthwise and crosswise

Spread a layer of butter on one side of each slice of bread. Top each with two pieces of salted anchovy. Serve.

To add a nice, acidic note and cut through the fat, garnish these with thin slivers of lemon segments.

APERITIVO
(DRINKS WITH SNACKS)

Romans rarely drink to excess; public intoxication is considered very poor form. Their secret to staying pleasantly buzzed without going over the edge? Always pairing drinks with food. Virtually every bar provides complimentary snacks with each alcoholic beverage, so whenever you order a drink, salted nuts, potato chips, *Pizzette* (page 186), or tiny sandwiches arrive at your table, too, at no extra cost.

In addition, many bars and pubs also offer a nightly *aperitivo*—think a sort of Italian happy hour—during which access to a buffet is included in the price of a drink. The *aperitivo* ritual migrated from northern Italy to Rome, where it has been embraced with gusto. Competition is fierce, especially in the student neighborhoods of San Lorenzo, Trastevere, and Piazza Bologna; most venues seek to entice customers with quantity over quality, rolling out flaccid crudités and veritable troughs of pasta salad and couscous. As much as we love carbs, the typical *aperitivo* snacks don't excite us, so we have imagined a few delicious, fresh Rome-inspired bites, including *Torta Rustica* (page 46), *Olive Marinate* (page 61), *Crostini con Burro e Alici* (page 62), *Bruschette con Carciofi, Limone, e Pecorino Romano* (page 66), and *Pizzette*, to serve alongside a pint of Italian craft beer (see page 230), an *apéritif*, or a cocktail (pages 227–243).

bruschette con carciofi, limone, e pecorino romano

BRUSCHETTA WITH ARTICHOKE, LEMON, AND PECORINO ROMANO

CARCIOFI ROMANESCHI, compact, greenish-purple globe artichokes, are ubiquitous in Roman markets from winter through early spring. The famous Roman thistle sets itself apart from the dozens of other artichoke species by having almost no choke and a distinct, delicate flavor. Despite their domination of the market stalls, Romans prepare them in just a few ways. *Carciofi alla giudia*, originating in the Jewish Ghetto, are trimmed, twice-fried, and seasoned with salt; *carciofi alla romana* are trimmed and cooked gently with olive oil, garlic, and herbs until dark and tender; and *carciofi infarinati*, floured and fried wedges, are a popular starter at Rome's top pizzerias. Here, we take the classic *carciofo alla romana* recipe a step further, mashing the cooked artichokes with lemon and Pecorino Romano to produce a chunky spread, ideal for slathering on any toasted rustic bread.

makes 10 **bruschette**

4 tender young artichokes, cleaned (see page 167)

Sea salt

¼ cup extra-virgin olive oil

1 garlic clove, smashed

Freshly ground black pepper

½ bunch fresh mint

½ bunch fresh flat-leaf parsley

½ cup grated Pecorino Romano

1 tablespoon lemon zest, plus more to taste

1½ tablespoons fresh lemon juice (from ½ lemon), plus more to taste

5 slices rustic bread, halved and toasted

Halve the artichokes, reserving the lemon water in which they were soaked. Using a teaspoon or a melon baller, scoop out and discard the fuzzy inner choke and trim off any rough, pointy bits. Slice the artichoke halves lengthwise in two.

Place the quartered artichokes and their peeled stems into a small pot. Season with salt and pepper to taste. Add the olive oil, garlic, mint, and parsley. Add the reserved lemon water to the pot to a depth of ½ inch. Cover the pot and cook over low heat until the artichokes are fork-tender, 20 to 25 minutes. Turn off the heat and allow the artichokes to cool, 15 minutes.

Transfer the artichokes and any remaining liquid to a medium bowl, along with the garlic and herbs, if desired. Add the Pecorino Romano, lemon zest, and lemon juice. Mash with a fork until the ingredients are incorporated and the artichokes have formed a chunky spread. Season to taste, adding more lemon juice as desired.

Spread on toast and serve immediately, garnished with additional lemon zest and pepper.

CLASSICS
AND
VARIATIONS

Rome's chefs and home cooks may all make a dish called *Cacio e Pepe* (page 74) or *Involtini di Manzo* (page 99), but each has his or her own personal approach. The classic dishes here are inspired by our favorite Roman restaurants, where well-loved recipes have something extra special that sets them apart in a city absolutely saturated with options. Our variations riff on traditional flavors or adapt local recipes, like Vito Bernabei's *Porchetta* (page 103), to a home kitchen.

CARBONARA

RECIPE DISCUSSIONS in any culture can inspire debate.
But bring up the subject of carbonara with a Roman and suggest an
ingredient or technique that diverges from his or her own, and you've
got a passionate fight on your hands. The fact is, there is no universal
or original recipe for carbonara. Generally, the pasta is spaghetti or
rigatoni. *Guanciale* (page 82) is the pork of choice for most, but some
do use pancetta. Almost every version uses black pepper, though some
contemporary chefs use white instead. Yolk-only versions are just as
common as whole egg; and some chefs use only Pecorino Romano,
while others mix it with Parmigiano-Reggiano.

Because there is no strict definition, every cook is free to make this
dish his or her own. And in Rome, that quest has become the object
of playful experimentation. We now have "carbonara pizza," ravioli
filled with carbonara sauce, and even a cocktail, *Carbonara Sour di
Co.So.* (page 228). The very idea of these innovations may make purists
shudder, just the way they must have when carbonara first burst onto
the scene in the mid-twentieth century.

The origins of the dish are as elusive as the perfect recipe. By most
accounts, it was first served in Rome in the late 1950s or early 1960s.
A popular legend holds that American soldiers invented it after World
War II, mixing their bacon rations with powdered eggs. It's a fun story,
but hard to prove. Other myths give the credit to *carbonari* (charcoal
makers), but our friend and scholar Jeremy Parzen has another
theory: the word *carbonari* had multiple meanings in nineteenth- and
twentieth-century Italy; the *Carboneria* was a Neapolitan secret society.
Does this fact, coupled with a cheese and beaten eggs dish in an early
nineteenth-century Neapolitan cookbook, mean a precursor to Rome's
carbonara was invented in Naples? It's impossible to say, which only
makes the debate over its components and origins more heated.

What we *can* say for sure is that carbonara is in an exciting
period of evolution at the moment, as new techniqes and ingredient
proportions are applied to a classic dish. The amount of *guanciale*
today's chefs use in their recipes has grown with respect to the past,

while it is increasingly common for the same chefs to discard some of the rendered *guanciale* fat in order to make the rich dish a touch lighter. Oh, the irony!

Of the many versions we enjoy, we find chef Flavio Di Maio's version at Flavio al Velavevodetto in Testaccio most satisfying because he transforms this heavy flavor bomb into a seemingly light and elegant condiment, relying on whole eggs and a splash of water to thin the normally dense sauce. We've adapted his recipe into a foolproof, consistently excellent version for the home kitchen (the "Zabaione Method"), but we've also provided an alternative method for preparing the dish so you can do a bit of your own experimenting with this ultimate classic.

rigatoni alla carbonara di flavio de maio

serves 4 to 6

1 teaspoon extra-virgin olive oil

7 ounces *Guanciale* (page 82), cut into approximately 1 × ½-inch strips

Sea salt

1 pound rigatoni

4 large eggs

1½ cups grated Pecorino Romano

Freshly ground black pepper

METHOD I : THE ZABAIONE METHOD (THE DOUBLE-BOILER METHOD)

Heat the olive oil in a small skillet over low heat. When the oil begins to shimmer, add the *guanciale*. Cook, stirring, until golden brown, about 8 minutes. Remove from the heat and allow the *guanciale* and its rendered fat to cool in the pan. If desired, remove some of the rendered fat and discard or use to make *Vodka al Guanciale* (page 228).

Meanwhile, bring a large pot of water to a rolling boil over high heat. Salt the water. When the salt has dissolved, add the pasta and cook until al dente (see page 34). Bring another large pot of water to a simmer over low heat. In a large stainless

RECIPE CONTINUES

You want the sauce to be loose enough to thoroughly coat the pasta, but not too runny. The trick to carbonara is to apply enough heat to the egg mixture to thicken it but not enough to make the egg scramble. When cooking the egg mixture in a pan, avoid nonstick materials and select a pan that conducts heat evenly.

steel bowl, or the top of a double boiler, beat together the eggs, 1 cup of the Pecorino Romano, a pinch of pepper, and ¼ cup water. Place the egg mixture over the simmering unsalted water, taking care to avoid direct contact between the bowl and the water. Whisk the egg mixture continually until it thickens and coats the back of a spoon. Remove from the double boiler. Add the *guanciale*, rendered fat, and al dente pasta to the egg mixture, stirring to coat.

Plate and sprinkle each portion with some of the remaining Pecorino Romano and pepper to taste. Serve immediately.

METHOD 2: IN THE PAN

Heat the olive oil in a large skillet over low heat. When the oil begins to shimmer, add the *guanciale*. Cook, stirring, until golden brown, about 8 minutes. Remove from the heat and allow the *guanciale* and its rendered fat to cool in the pan. If desired, remove some of the rendered fat and discard or use to make *Vodka al Guanciale* (page 228).

Meanwhile, bring a large pot of water to a rolling boil over high heat. Salt the water. When the salt has dissolved, add the pasta and cook until al dente (see page 34).

While the pasta is cooking, in a medium bowl, beat together the eggs, 1 cup of the Pecorino Romano, a pinch of pepper, and ¼ cup water. Add the egg mixture to the pan with the cooked *guanciale*.

When the pasta is cooked, drain it and add the pasta to the pan and stir continuously over low heat, slowly heating the egg mixuture, but taking care not to scramble it. When the egg begins to adhere to the pasta and to the sides of the pan, turn off the heat.

Plate and sprinkle each portion with some of the remaining Pecorino Romano and pepper to taste. Serve immediately.

cacio e pepe di leonardo vignoli

LEONARDO VIGNOLI'S *CACIO E PEPE*

CACIO is the local Roman dialect word for Pecorino Romano, a sheep's-milk cheese made in the region since ancient times. Like *carbonara* (see page 70), *cacio e pepe* is a relative newcomer to the Roman repertoire, first appearing in the mid-twentieth century. Pasta is tossed with an emulsified sauce of Pecorino Romano and black pepper that is bound by starchy pasta cooking water. Depending on the cook, the results range from dry to juicy. We love Leonardo Vignoli's saucy version at Cesare al Casaletto. He uses ice in a hot pan to obtain a creamy sauce, but we have adapted his recipe to obtain more consistent results in a home kitchen. Finely grated Pecorino Romano and very hot water are essential to a smooth sauce, while fresh, coarsely ground black pepper gives flavor and texture. The most important component of a flawless *cacio e pepe*, however, is speed. If the water cools before melting the cheese, the sauce will clump.

serves 4 to 6

Sea salt

1 pound spaghetti or *tonnarelli*

2 cups finely grated Pecorino Romano

2 teaspoons freshly ground black pepper, plus more to taste

Bring a large pot of water to a rolling boil over high heat. Salt the water. When the salt has dissolved, add the pasta and cook until al dente (see page 34).

Meanwhile, in a large bowl, combine 1½ cups of the Pecorino Romano, the pepper, and a small ladle of pasta cooking water. Using the back of a large wooden spoon, mix vigorously and quickly to form a paste.

When the pasta is cooked, use a large strainer to remove it from the cooking water and quickly add it to the sauce in the bowl, keeping the cooking water boiling on the stove. Toss vigorously, adjusting with additional hot water a tablespoon or two at a time as necessary to melt the cheese and to obtain a juicy sauce that completely coats the pasta.

Plate and sprinkle each portion with some of the remaining Pecorino Romano and pepper to taste. Serve immediately.

Some cooks toast the peppercorns, but we prefer untoasted pepper.

spaghetti alla gricia di claudio gargioli

CLAUDIO GARGIOLI'S *SPAGHETTI ALLA GRICIA*

GRICIA is sometimes described as *carbonara* (see page 70) minus the egg, or *amatriciana* (see page 77) without the tomato, but such descriptions fail to acknowledge that *spaghetti alla gricia* is a pure and satisfying dish all its own. It's likely that some form of *gricia* came before those others, introduced by immigrants arriving from the Apennines, and was modified when it reached the Italian capital. In our opinion, you can find the finest incarnation at Armando al Pantheon, a trattoria located a mere hundred feet from the Pantheon. When Armando Gargioli opened this spot in 1961, the tables were filled with the city's politicians and poets. Today, this audience shares space with hungry tourists, too, who come to one of the few remaining trattorias in central Rome where high standards of quality are maintained. The secret to Armando's *gricia*, now dutifully reproduced by his son Claudio, is white wine, which infuses the savory *guanciale*.

serves 4 to 6

Sea salt

1 pound spaghetti (Claudio likes Martelli brand)

1 teaspoon extra-virgin olive oil

7 ounces *Guanciale* (page 82), cut into 1½ × ½-inch strips

½ cup white wine

1 cup grated Pecorino Romano

Freshly ground black pepper

Bring a large pot of water to a rolling boil over high heat. Salt the water. When the salt has dissolved, add the pasta and cook until very al dente (see page 34). Drain, reserving the cooking water.

Heat the olive oil in a large skillet over low heat. When the oil begins to shimmer, add the *guanciale* and cook, stirring, until golden brown, about 8 minutes. Add the white wine and cook until the alcohol aroma dissipates, about a minute more.

Add a small ladle of the pasta cooking water to the skillet with the *guanciale* and bring to a simmer. Add the pasta and another small ladle of its cooking water to the pan with the *guanciale*. Cook over medium-high heat, stirring vigorously, until a thick sauce forms, adding more water if necessary to achieve the desired consistency.

Remove the skillet from the heat, add ¾ cup of the Pecorino Romano, and mix thoroughly. Season to taste.

Plate and sprinkle each portion with some of the remaining Pecorino Romano and pepper to taste. Serve immediately.

bombolotti all'amatriciana di roscioli

ROSCIOLI'S *BOMBOLOTTI ALL'AMATRICIANA*

AS WITH every Roman recipe, *l'amatriciana* (or *la matriciana* to some) sparks lively discussion. Does it include onion or garlic, *guanciale* or pancetta, chile or black pepper? Even its origins are undocumented and therefore hotly debated. Amatrice, a village northeast of Rome, claims it originated there; others say the name refers to the *matrice*, or brand, that was pressed into *guanciale*. We may never know, but it is currently a Roman classic. We prefer chef Nabil Hadj Hassen's version served at Roscioli, a modern restaurant and wine bar in the historic center, and have adapted it here. Departing from tradition, Hassen uses shallots instead of onion and introduces big cubes of crispy *guanciale*, all served with tubular *bombolotti*, which often hide savory bits of *guanciale* inside.

serves 4 to 6

3 teaspoons extra-virgin olive oil

7 ounces *Guanciale* (page 82), cut into ½-inch cubes

2 medium shallots, minced

Sea salt

1 (28-ounce) can whole tomatoes (we like San Marzano), hand crushed

1 pound *bombolotti* (also called *mezze maniche*) or other short, tubular, ridged pasta

¾ cup grated Pecorino Romano

Heat 1 teaspoon of olive oil in a small skillet over low heat. When the oil begins to shimmer, add the *guanciale*. Cook, stirring, until golden brown and crisp, about 10 minutes. Remove the pan from the heat and set aside.

Heat the remaining olive oil in a large skillet over medium-low heat. Add the shallots and season with salt. Cook until softened, about 5 minutes, then add the tomatoes and increase the heat to medium. Cook for about 15 minutes, or until the sauce has reduced slightly and tastes less acidic. Add the *guanciale* and rendered fat to the pan with the tomatoes.

While the sauce is cooking, bring a large pot of water to a rolling boil over high heat. Salt the water. When the salt has dissolved, add the pasta. Cook until very al dente (see page 34), then drain, reserving the cooking water.

Add the pasta to the tomato sauce in the skillet and toss to coat. Add enough reserved pasta cooking water to nearly cover the pasta. Simmer, stirring, adding more cooking water as needed, until the pasta is al dente. Remove the skillet from the heat, add ½ cup of the Pecorino Romano, and mix well. Season with salt to taste.

Plate and sprinkle each portion with some of the remaining Pecorino Romano. Serve immediately.

amatriciana estiva

SUMMER AMATRICIANA

AMATRICIANA ESTIVA, or summer *amatriciana*, is a phrase that has been popping up on trattoria menus all over town for a few years now. Some claim their version of the dish is lighter than the classic because they use less *guanciale* or drain off some of the rendered fat. Others don't reduce the fat at all, and just replace canned tomatoes with seasonal summer ones. We like a version somewhere between the two, and recommend using thin pieces of *guanciale* and, of course, incorporating fresh summer tomatoes instead of canned.

serves 4 to 6

1 teaspoon extra-virgin olive oil

3 ounces *Guanciale* (page 82), cut into matchsticks

1 garlic clove, smashed

1½ pounds cherry tomatoes, halved

6 to 8 fresh basil leaves

Sea salt

1 pound *bombolotti* or another short, tubular, ridged pasta

½ cup grated Pecorino Romano

Heat the olive oil in a large skillet over low heat. When the oil begins to shimmer, add the *guanciale*. Cook, stirring, until golden brown and very crisp, about 10 minutes. Using a slotted spoon, transfer to a paper towel to drain. Remove half the rendered fat from the pan and discard or reserve for another use like *Vodka al Guanciale* (page 228). Add the garlic to the pan. Cook until the garlic just turns golden, about 10 minutes, then add the tomatoes. Increase the heat to medium and cook until the tomatoes lose their shape, about 10 minutes, then stir in the basil.

Meanwhile, bring a large pot of water to a rolling boil over high heat. Salt the water. When the salt has dissolved, add the pasta. Cook until very al dente (see page 34), then drain, reserving the cooking water.

Add the pasta to the sauce in the skillet and stir to coat. Add enough reserved pasta cooking water to nearly cover the pasta. Simmer, adding more cooking water as needed. When the pasta is al dente, remove the skillet from the heat. Add ¼ cup of the Pecorino Romano and mix well. Add half the *guanciale* and stir well. Season to taste.

Plate and sprinkle each portion with some of the remaining Pecorino Romano and *guanciale*. Serve immediately.

Prosciutto
Cotto Piacentino
€ 35.00 kg

Guanciale
umbro
majali bradi

Pancetta
di Cormons
suino pesante

Pancetta
Umbra
maiale bradi   kg
                     42.00

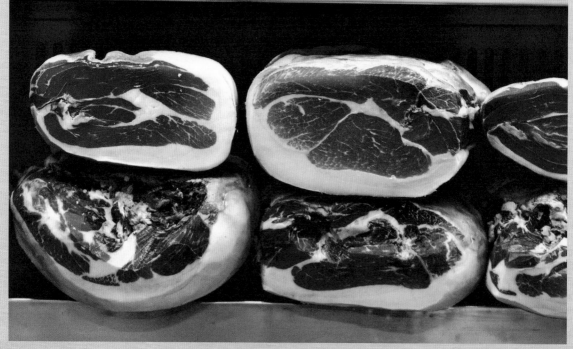

GUANCIALE

GUANCIALE, whole cured pork jowl, is a fundamental element of the *cucina romana*. Its rendered fat lends flavor and viscosity to classic pasta dishes like *Carbonara* (see page 70), *Amatriciana* (see page 77), and *Gricia* (see page 76).

In Rome, whole *guanciali* hang above deli counters at *alimentari* (small groceries) and at supermarkets; customers can order slabs sliced from the roughly triangular cured cheeks.

Guanciale is produced all over central Italy, especially in the regions of Lazio, Umbria, and Abruzzo, and recipes vary from producer to producer. Some cure their cheeks with *peperoncino*, herbs, or spices, but we prefer simple salt and pepper—a favorite of Rome's traditional cooks and chefs. It has become more available outside of Italy in recent years, but can be pricey. You can substitute cured pork belly, like unsmoked pancetta or bacon, but bear in mind that they aren't exactly interchangeable, as *guanciale* is quite a bit fattier. Alternatively, you can make *guanciale* from scratch using our recipe (see page 82). It is a fairly simple process that takes a little over a month.

Now here's our disclaimer about making *guanciale* at home: the most important factor to consider when getting started is food safety. Use gloves, food-safe surfaces, and, perhaps most important for beginners, pink salt—a curing mixture that will safeguard your *guanciale* from dangerous bacterial growth while also preserving the pinkish color of the meat. Full dislosure: Roman *norcini* (pork butchers), including our favorite local expert, Vito Bernabei, famous for his *Porchetta* (page 103), usually don't use curing salts or additives when making whole muscle cures and the incidence of botulism is extremely low, but it would be irresponsible of us to not at least give you a warning. Pink salt is sold in specialty food stores and some supermarkets, but fresh pork jowls are a bit harder to come by. You may need to reach out to a specialty butcher or a local hog farmer, or search online for sources (see Resources, page 249). Look for jowls from heritage breeds raised ethically, which have been fed a complete diet; the flavor and quality of the fat really is superior.

Our source for *guanciale* in Rome is Azienda Agricola Fanelli. They shared their approach to *guanciale* making with us and stressed the importance of using meat from animals that had eaten a natural diet. They feed their happy pigs a mixture of grains and vegetable scraps. The precise weight of each pork jowl varies, so we have given approximate quantities, which can be tweaked according to your needs. The Fanellis eyeball their ingredients, but here are some guidelines.

il guanciale di alessandro fanelli

ALESSANDRO FANELLI'S GUANCIALE

makes 1 cured pork jowl

1 pound (450 grams) fresh pork jowl, trimmed and glands removed

1 tablespoon (15 grams) high-quality sea salt (2 to 3% pork weight)

Pinch (1½ grams) of pink salt (.25% pork weight)

2 tablespoons (15 grams) freshly ground black pepper

The weight of your pork jowl may differ slightly. Aim for 2 to 3% of its weight in sea salt and .25% of its weight in pink salt.

Rinse the jowl and pat it dry.

Combine the sea salt and pink salt in a large resealable plastic bag. Add the jowl and massage the cure into the meat, distributing it evenly. Seal the bag and put it on the bottom shelf of the refrigerator for 4 to 7 days, or until the meat stiffens, flipping it daily.

Remove the meat from the bag. Wipe the meat with a damp rag, then pat it dry. Using a sharp knife, carefully make a hole in the small end of the jowl. Rub the pepper onto the surface of the meat, coating it thoroughly. Weigh the meat and make a note of its weight in grams.

Run kitchen twine through the hole in the jowl to form a loop, then hang it in a cool, humid place with good ventilation, such as a shed. The *guanciale* is ready when it has lost roughly 30 percent of its weight and is firm but not hard, 2 to 4 weeks. Take it down and weigh it at the 1½ week mark to check its progress. When you're ready to cook with it, trim the peppery outer layer, taking care to leave plenty of fat on the exterior. You only want to clean off the pepper crust and any excess tissue, not remove the thick exterior fat layer. That's the good stuff!

picchiapò

SIMMERED BEEF WITH TOMATO AND ONION

TRADITIONALLY SPEAKING, *picchiapò* is a dish that emerged to make the most of leftover cooked meat. As such, recipes vary from cook to cook, and even from day to day. Ours is inspired by Sergio and Mara Esposito's version at Mordi e Vai, a stall in the Testaccio Market. The Espositos serve sandwiches filled with Roman classics such as *allesso di scottona*, a simmered beef dish. They cook their leftover *allesso* in a spicy, oniony tomato sauce, along with vegetables, creating the dish *picchiapò*. To make it from scratch at home, you can cook beef specifically for this purpose, or just start with simmered leftovers. Serve it on its own or on a *Ciabattina* (page 192), as the Espositos do. For more flavorful beef, salt the meat with kosher salt at least 4 hours and up to 24 hours before cooking.

serves 4 to 6

1 pound beef shin or trim, nerve removed, salted in advance

1 cup dry white wine

2 carrots

3 onions

10 whole black peppercorns

3 whole cloves

2 tablespoons extra-virgin olive oil

Sea salt

1 tablespoon fresh marjoram

Pinch of *peperoncino* or red pepper flakes

1 (14-ounce) can crushed tomatoes

Place the salted beef in a large pot with water to cover. Slowly bring the water to a gentle simmer over low heat, skimming off any foam that rises to the top. Then add the wine, carrots, 2 of the onions, the peppercorns, and the cloves. Cook at a low simmer until the beef is fork-tender, about 2 hours. Transfer the meat to a plate and shred it with tongs or two forks. Coarsely chop the cooked carrots and set aside.

Heat the olive oil in a large skillet over low heat. Meanwhile, coarsely chop the remaining onion. When the oil begins to shimmer, add the onion and cook until translucent, about 10 minutes. Season with salt, then add the marjoram and *peperoncino* and cook until fragrant, about 30 seconds. Add the tomatoes and cook until the sauce has reduced slightly and become less acidic, about 15 minutes. Add the shredded beef and carrots. Stir well, then cook for 15 minutes more to allow the sauce to come together and reduce slightly.

Serve immediately as a stand-alone dish, or use as a sandwich filling on a soft bun or crusty bread.

pollo alla romana

CHICKEN WITH TOMATOES AND BELL PEPPERS

POLLO ALLA ROMANA is a dish long associated with *Ferragosto*, the August 15 holiday that celebrates the Assumption of the Virgin Mary. Local chefs and home cooks alike now serve it all summer long when temperatures rise and they want to make food they can prepare in the relatively cooler mornings and serve lukewarm at lunchtime. We recommend serving *pollo alla romana* as the main dish in a meal that begins with *Fettuccine con Rigaglie di Pollo* (page 130), which is how it has been enjoyed at *Ferragosto* for ages. For a more delicious final product, season the chicken with salt at least 6 hours and up to 24 hours before cooking. In Rome, it is common to use a mixture of red and yellow bell peppers. This color motif is popular, also seen in the colors of the city flag and AS Roma, one of Rome's two professional soccer teams.

serves 4

3 tablespoons extra-virgin olive oil

1 whole chicken, salted in advance and cut into 8 pieces

2 yellow onions, cut into ¼-inch-thick slices

3 bell peppers, seeded and cut into 1-inch slices

2 garlic cloves, smashed

½ cup dry white wine

1 tablespoon fresh marjoram

1 (14-ounce) can whole or crushed tomatoes

To prevent the breast from drying out, you may want to remove it from the pan before the legs and thighs.

Heat the olive oil in a large skillet over medium heat. When the oil begins to shimmer, add the chicken, skin-side down, and cook for 8 to 10 minutes, until it is browned on all sides, adjusting the heat as necessary to prevent burning. Reduce the heat to low, remove the chicken, and set aside.

Add the onions, bell peppers, and garlic to the same pan and cook until the onions and peppers have softened, about 10 minutes. Add the wine, increase the heat to medium, and scrape up all the browned bits from the bottom of the pan. Once the alcohol aroma dissipates, about a minute, add the marjoram and tomatoes. Return the chicken to the pan and add enough water to submerge it halfway. Cook, stirring occasionally, for 30 minutes more, until the chicken is tender and nearly falling away from the bone and the sauce is thick and deep red, but not dry. If the sauce becomes too dry, add a bit more water.

Serve immediately as a stand-alone dish. You can also reheat deboned leftovers to serve with crusty bread or on Passi's *Ciabattine* (page 192).

ajo, ojo, peperoncino, e pomodori arrostiti

GARLIC, OIL, *PEPERONCINO*, AND ROASTED TOMATOES

THE BASIS of this recipe is *ajo, ojo, e peperoncino*, a spicy classic dish in which spaghetti is tossed with garlic and chile cooked in olive oil. Local lore holds that this meal, which is also called *pasta dei cornuti*, "cuckold's pasta," is served by cheating wives who, otherwise occupied, don't have time to prepare a proper dinner while their husbands are away at work. Misogynist stereotypes aside, the trick to this dish is uniting and intensifying all the flavors so you're not left with a watery mess. You achieve this by simmering some pasta cooking water with the garlic, oil, and *peperoncino*, concentrating the starch and emulsifying the flavors, then adding the pasta to absorb the flavors in the pan. *Ajo, ojo, e peperoncino* is served either ungarnished, with a bit of chopped parsley, or even with fried bread crumbs—as with all classics, the individual tastes of the cook prevail. Our variation incorporates oven-roasted tomatoes, which introduce a concentrated acidity and subtly sweet counterpoint to the spicy, garlicky pasta.

serves 4 to 6

FOR THE ROASTED TOMATOES

3 pounds small plum tomatoes (about 24 tomatoes)

2 large pinches of sea salt

Leaves from 6 sprigs fresh thyme (optional)

Olive oil for preserving, if using (see sidebar, opposite)

FOR THE PASTA

Sea salt

1 pound spaghetti

⅓ cup extra-virgin olive oil

2 garlic cloves, smashed

1 *peperoncino* or 1 teaspoon red pepper flakes

Make the tomatoes: Preheat the oven to 225°F. Line a baking sheet with parchment paper.

Bring a large pot of water to a boil over high heat. Meanwhile, hull the tomatoes and cut an X in the other end. Place the tomatoes in the boiling water for 10 to 15 seconds, then remove to an ice bath. Allow to sit for 1 minute, then drain.

Peel the tomatoes with a paring knife, halve them, and place them cut-side up on the prepared baking sheet. Sprinkle with the salt and thyme leaves (if using). Bake for 2 to 2½ hours, until the tomatoes shrivel and shrink by about half. Remove from the oven and allow to cool completely.

Make the pasta: Bring a large pot of water to a rolling boil over high heat. Salt the water. When the salt has dissolved, add the pasta and cook until al dente (see page 34).

While the pasta cooks, heat the olive oil in a large skillet over low heat. When the oil begins to shimmer, add the garlic and cook until it just turns golden, about 5 minutes. Add the

If you don't use the tomatoes immediately, or don't use them all, layer them in a wide-mouthed jar or bowl with herbs and cover them with extra-virgin olive oil to preserve them. They will keep in the refrigerator for up to 3 weeks, though the olive oil may turn cloudy. Bring the tomatoes to room temperature before serving.

peperoncino and cook until fragrant, about 30 seconds. Discard the garlic, or leave it in. (Romans do either.)

Once the pasta is al dente, drain, reserving the cooking water. Add the pasta and some cooking water to the pan with the garlic and *peperoncino,* and stir well to coat. If the sauce is too dry, add a bit more cooking water and toss vigorously.

Plate and top each serving with a few roasted tomatoes. Serve immediately.

ROMAN CULINARY CANON

A LOT OF THINGS in Rome are unpredictable. Perhaps the Forum will be closed for an emergency union meeting, or maybe the 75 bus will pass three times in ten minutes and then fail to reappear for over an hour. There are other things in the Italian capital, on the other hand, that you can always count on. Among them is the availability of gnocchi. The phrase *giovedì gnocchi* ("gnocchi on Thursdays") is, among all the elements of Rome's cultural canon, the most reliable.

Every Thursday, home cooks and trattorias serve the local potato dumpling, sparingly dressed with a tomato-based sauce. Some locals assert that the tradition of eating gnocchi on Thursday stems from the need to eat something rib-sticking before lean, meatless Fridays, as mandated by the Catholic calendar. That claim isn't altogether logical unless the gnocchi in question are heavy and pasty, which is the exact opposite of a good gnocco's desired texture. More likely, the tradition derives from Thursdays being treated in a festive manner, calling for pasta made with eggs, potatoes, or both in preparations that were richer than the simple flour-and-water standard.

Whatever the reason for the *giovedì gnocchi* tradition, the fish dishes that define Fridays are easier to decode. Because of the customary meat prohibition that day, restaurants and home cooks everywhere prepare fish soup, *baccalà* (salt cod), and other seafood. On Friday mornings, many delis, market stalls, and supermarkets prominently display desalted cod.

Of all the dishes on Rome's traditional dining calendar , Thursday and Friday traditions are the most closely followed today. That's not to say that other traditional foods have totally vanished, but many are now served all week long, rather than remaining married to a single day of service. Weekends were once given over to labor-intensive dishes: *Trippa alla Romana* (page 142) was a Saturday tradition, while Sundays were dedicated to *suppli* or fresh pastas like fettuccine and *lasagne*. Monday was the day for simmered meats, followed by Tuesday's fish or pasta with chickpeas. Wednesday's dishes were pasta with beans or *Coda alla Vaccinara* (page 147), braised oxtail, which led to Thursday, when gnocchi might be dressed with deeply flavored oxtail sauce left over from the previous day.

gnocchi di patate di arcangelo dandini

ARCANGELO DANDINI'S POTATO GNOCCHI

THURSDAYS ARE traditionally dedicated to potato gnocchi; they should not be confused with *gnocchi alla romana*: baked disks of semolina, butter, milk, and Parmigiano-Reggiano. Gnocchi master Arcangelo Dandini of L'Arcangelo makes gnocchi that are exquisitely pillowy and delicate, a texture he achieves by using a ricer instead of a food mill. To avoid heavy or gluey results, he recommends using floury potatoes grown in dry terrain. The ones he likes grow in the arid fields of the central Apennine Mountains, but you can use whatever dry, floury potatoes you can find. The final dish should be dressed sparingly, ideally with a bit of sauce from *Amatriciana* (see page 77), *Involtini* (see page 99), or *Coda alla Vaccinara* (page 147).

serves 4 to 6

1 pound dry, floury
potatoes, such as russets

Sea salt

1⅓ cups all-purpose flour,
plus more for dusting

Pinch of freshly grated
nutmeg

Don't let the potatoes cool off too much. They should still be steaming when you peel them. If you wish, wear gloves to avoid burning your fingers!

Place the potatoes in a large pot. Add cold water to cover and salt the water. Bring to a boil over medium-high heat and cook the potatoes until fork-tender. Drain and allow to cool slightly, just a few minutes. Peel the potatoes with a knife, then pass them through a ricer onto a well-floured surface. Form the riced potatoes into a pile and make a well in the middle.

Add the flour, nutmeg, and a pinch of salt to the well, then mix by hand, working from the edges into the center to gradually incorporate the ingredients into a dough. Knead the dough just until incorporated. Allow to rest at room temperature for about 30 minutes.

On a lightly floured surface, form a fistful of dough into a log roughly ¾ inch in diameter. Using a knife, cut the log crosswise into ½-inch-long pieces. Set aside on a lightly floured surface, spaced apart to prevent sticking. Repeat with the remaining dough.

Bring a large pot of water to a rolling boil over high heat. Salt the water. When the salt dissolves, add the gnocchi in batches and cook for an additional 20 seconds after they float to the surface. Drain the gnocchi and transfer to a pan with the sauce of your choice. Warm over medium heat and gently stir to coat thoroughly with the sauce. Plate and serve immediately.

agnello brodettato

LAMB IN EGG AND HERB SAUCE

THIS SPRING DISH used to be made using whole lambs or kids, but now cooks use smaller proportions. *Brodettato* refers to the dish's most critical element, the broth, which binds it together. Salt the lamb with kosher salt 24 hours in advance.

serves 4 to 6

FOR THE LAMB BROTH

A few lamb bones

1 carrot

1 onion

1 celery stalk

FOR THE LAMB

2 ounces prosciutto fat, finely chopped, or 2 tablespoons extra-virgin olive oil

3½ pounds bone-in lamb shoulder or shank, salted in advance and cut into 2-inch pieces

All-purpose flour, for dredging

1 garlic clove, smashed

1 onion, chopped

Sea salt

1 cup dry white wine

4 large egg yolks

3 tablespoons fresh lemon juice (from 1 lemon), plus more to taste

Leaves from 3 sprigs fresh mint, chopped

Leaves from 6 sprigs fresh flat-leaf parsley, chopped

Leaves from 3 sprigs fresh marjoram, chopped

Freshly ground black pepper

Make the broth: Put the lamb bones and trimmings in a large pot and add cold water to cover. Bring to a simmer over low heat. Skim. Add the carrot, onion, and celery. Simmer for at least 4 hours and up to 6 hours, occasionally skimming off any foam that rises to the surface.

After you have made the broth, make the lamb: In a large pot, render the prosciutto fat over low heat. Dredge the lamb in flour, shaking off any excess, and add it to the pan. Cook until browned, 3 to 5 minutes. Remove and set aside.

Add the garlic and onion to the same pan. Season with salt and cook over medium heat until the onion is translucent and soft, about 10 minutes. Add the wine, scraping up any browned bits from the bottom of the pan. Once the alcohol aroma dissipates, about a minute, return the meat to the pan. Add enough lamb broth so that the meat is almost submerged and simmer, partially covered, until fork-tender but not quite falling off the bone, about 1½ hours. Add more broth during cooking as necessary to keep the lamb mostly submerged.

Just before serving, whisk together the egg yolks, 3 tablespoons lemon juice, and herbs. Temper the egg mixture by stirring in a few ounces of the hot lamb broth. Add the tempered egg mixture to the pan with the lamb and reheat gently while stirring. Remove the pan from the heat. Season with salt, pepper, and remaining lemon juice, to taste. Serve immediately.

WHO REALLY
COOKS IN ROME?

IN ITALY, perhaps more so than anywhere else on earth, romantic notions of a timeless past persist. In spite of plenty of evidence to the contrary, visitors and locals alike still fantasize that Rome's kitchens are populated by plump *nonnas* hard at work prepping, cooking, and cleaning. Sure, there are still some family-run institutions in which multiple generations toil at the stove, but that's not necessarily the norm, and a survey of Roman food culture would be remiss in omitting the key players who really keep the city's restaurant kitchens running.

Immigrants, primarily men from South Asia and North Africa, are the unacknowledged anchors of Rome's dining scene. With fewer and fewer young Romans signing on for the poorly compensated and grueling job of restaurant work, immigrants have filled kitchen positions at every level, from dishwashers to head chefs. Many never emerge from anonymity, thwarted by legal status, xenophobia, or poverty, but they remain the undercelebrated backbone of a tough business. Rome's hotel kitchens, restaurants, trattorias, osterias, and pizzerias couldn't thrive without them.

involtini di manzo

BEEF ROLLS

COOK ONCE, eat twice. It's an idea any busy home cook can get behind, and it's what we love about *involtini di manzo*. As these meat rolls cook, their juices mingle with the tomato sauce and a few hearty bits get left behind, too. So hold on to that leftover sauce and use it to dress pasta a day or two later. We like it with rigatoni, spaghetti, or *Gnocchi di Patate* (page 95).

makes 6 involtini, plus 2 cups sauce for pasta

1 pound rump roast, cut into six equal slices

Sea salt

6 thin slices prosciutto

1 carrot, julienned

1 celery stalk, julienned

2 tablespoons extra-virgin olive oil

1 garlic clove, smashed

1 (28-ounce) can whole peeled tomatoes

1 cup dry white wine

Freshly ground black pepper

Lay the slices of beef flat on your work surface and season with salt on both sides. Place 1 piece of prosciutto over each slice of meat, followed by 3 or 4 sticks each of carrot and celery at one short end of the meat. Roll the meat around the vegetables, forming a medium-tight *involtino*. Use kitchen twine or a couple of toothpicks inserted flush with the meat to keep the roll closed.

Heat the olive oil in a small skillet over medium heat. When the oil begins to shimmer, add the *involtini* and brown them on all sides, about 5 minutes total. Remove the rolls from the pan and set aside.

Add the garlic to the same pan and cook, stirring occasionally, until it just turns golden, about 5 minutes. Stir in the tomatoes. Add the wine and cook until the alcohol aroma dissipates, about a minute. When the sauce begins to simmer, return the *involtini* to the pan. The meat should be mostly covered by the tomato sauce. Cook, covered, until the meat is fork-tender, about 1½ hours, checking occasionally to be sure the meat is at least two-thirds submerged and adding water if necessary. Season with salt and pepper. Serve immediately or allow the dish to rest in the refrigerator for up to 3 days to allow the flavors to develop.

HOLIDAY DISHES

ALTHOUGH ROME is increasingly secular, holidays are an opportunity for friends and families to gather around the table and share a common cuisine. Some saint-related feast days still hold real culinary significance. The Feast of Saint Joseph on March 19 is celebrated with *bignè di San Giuseppe*, fried, cream-filled pastries. On June 24, the Feast of Saint John, old-school trattorias serve snails cooked with garlic, anchovy, tomato, and mint. On *Ferragosto*, August 15, Romans celebrate the Feast of the Assumption with picnics of prosciutto and melon or figs, *Fettuccine con Rigaglie di Pollo* (page 130), and *Pollo alla Romana* (page 89).

The year's culinary festivities culminate with Christmas feasts. Christmas Eve is celebrated with a seafood meal including anchovies, eels, and salt cod. On Christmas Day, meat-filled pasta is served in broth, followed by capon, lamb, dandelion greens, and cardoons. Fresh fruit and *pangiallo*, a dense cake of honey, nuts, raisins, and spices like cloves, nutmeg, and cinnamon, conclude the meal.

Carnival sweets like *frappe* and *Castagnole* (page 207) are the first holiday foods of the New Year, followed by *maritozzi quaresimali*, a candied fruit– and pine nut–studded version of our simple breakfast *maritozzi* (see page 216), at Lent. The spring lamb slaughter, a ritual that has been carried out for centuries, culminates in Easter and Passover meals shared at the family table. Neither Catholic nor Jewish culture is in the business of wasting such a sacrificial animal, so alongside the meat, they serve sautéed innards, fried brains, and even roasted heads.

At Passover, Roman Jews eat matzo-based desserts like *Pizzarelle* (page 124), while Libyan Jews make a similar, honey-soaked fried matzo dumpling called *ajij*. At Catholic tables, the Easter meal begins with a plate of mixed appetizers featuring a hard-boiled egg, a symbol of life, perfection, and resurrection. Easter meals conclude with yeasted breads called *colombe*, not vastly different from the Christmas panettone, though dove-shaped rather than round.

porchetta di vito bernabei

VITO BERNABEI'S *PORCHETTA*

VITO BERNABEI'S *porchetta*—deboned, slow-roasted pork—is a thing of beauty. This third-generation *norcino* (pork butcher) makes his using the belly and loin of pigs he sources from small farms near his shop in Marino Laziale, thirteen miles southeast of Rome. He massages the meat with salt, herbs, and spices, sews it closed into a thick roll, and roasts it slowly to produce a spectacularly succulent and flavorful *porchetta*. Finding a belly and loin cut can be difficult in the United States—plus it produces an enormous amount of food and challenges the dimensions of most kitchen ovens. But you can still make roasted pork in Bernabei's style by substituting a deboned pork shoulder. The process is relatively easy. Just marinate the meat overnight, cook low and slow, and you'll have a juicy meal to look forward to.

serves 10

1 (6- to 7-pound) deboned, skin-on pork shoulder

3 tablespoons kosher salt

1 tablespoon freshly ground black pepper

4 garlic cloves, mashed to a paste

1 tablespoon chopped fresh rosemary

1 tablespoon *peperoncino* or red pepper flakes

2 teaspoons fennel pollen or ground fennel seeds

———

The skin should be bubbly and blistered, like pork rinds.

———

On a clean, dry work surface, score the pork skin in a diamond pattern (or have your butcher do it for you), then flip the pork skin-side down. Massage the salt into the meat, then dust it with the pepper, garlic, rosemary, *peperoncino*, and fennel pollen.

Roll the pork tightly, with the skin facing out, and tie it securely with kitchen twine. Marinate in the refrigerator, uncovered, for at least 6 hours or overnight, allowing the skin to dry out.

Remove the pork from the refrigerator 1½ to 2 hours before you cook it. Preheat the oven to 195°F.

Bake the *porchetta* until fork-tender, about 5 to 6 hours, then increase the oven temperature to 500°F and cook for 15 to 20 minutes more to crisp the skin.

Remove from the oven and allow to rest for at least 45 minutes, then slice and serve.

CUCINA EBRAICA

There may be only thirteen thousand Jews in Rome—a city of over 4 million—but the community's food culture looms large. Due in part to three centuries of isolation in a walled Ghetto, Roman Jews crafted a distinct cuisine called the *cucina ebraica romanesca*, which coaxes intense flavor from paltry resources. In the 1960s, Rome's small community was also enriched by thousands of Jews arriving from Libya who brought new customs and flavors to a historic tradition.

GHETTO CUISINE

THE FIRST Italian Ghetto was built in Venice in 1516. The
unfortunate European custom of confining Jews to segregated quarters
spread through Italy, and in 1555, the Roman Ghetto was established
by papal decree. Pope Paul IV relegated the city's Jewish population
to a squalid, fire-prone neighborhood on the banks of the Tiber River.
Buildings were crowded and claustrophobic as it was, but as the
population grew, precarious upper stories teetered above the already
decrepit ones. The Ghetto was liberated in 1870, only after the pope
lost his political authority in Rome. During those three centuries of
crowded isolation and unrelenting persecution, a distinct Jewish culture
and cuisine emerged.

Naturally, the cuisine of Rome's Jewish community was shaped
by the rules of Kashrut, the religion's dietary laws. But it was also
influenced by Rome's geography and the seasonal produce, both
cultivated and wild, that grew on its rolling hills and in its swampy
valleys. Spanish Jews, arriving in Rome from Spain and southern Italy
in the fifteenth century, introduced new ingredients like spices and
almond paste and preparations like escabeche (cooking and marinating;
see *Concia*, page 109). By the sixteenth century, Italian and Spanish
Jews were connected by religious bonds, as well as by the common
Ghetto experience, and their married cuisines mirrored the paltry
resources of the community.

The main ingredients during the Ghetto period were cheap and
abundant items like globe artichokes and lettuces, as well as salt cod,
Tiber fish, poor cuts of meat, and offal. *Pesce azzurro*, an oily category
of fish including mackerel, sardines, and anchovies, were sold at the
fish market inside the crumbling ruins of the Portico d'Ottavia on
the edge of the Ghetto, and used for flavorful soups. What meat was
available was simmered for hours to mellow its toughness. Such slow-
cooked meat dishes called *stracotti* are still common on Roman Jewish
tables. Frying was also a popular cooking method and even today,
Roman Jewish homes and restaurants serve *Pezzetti Fritti* (see page 58),
fried brains, *Filetti di Baccalà* (page 57), and twice-fried *carciofi alla
giudia* (Jewish-style artichokes).

King Victor Emanuel II liberated the Ghetto in 1870 and restored freedom to its inhabitants. In subsequent decades, the Ghetto's labyrinth of dilapidated buildings was razed, paving the way for an elegant, modern district. Today, kosher businesses, contemporary art galleries, prestigious apartments, and a glorious modern synagogue rise above the ruins. But the flavors of the Ghetto survive on the menus of restaurants like Nonna Betta, named for owner Umberto Pavoncello's grandmother. There, and in the few remaining Jewish homes in the fashionable rebuilt district, an ancient cuisine persists and testifies to the vanished zone and to the continuity of its people.

concia

FRIED AND MARINATED ZUCCHINI

CONCIA, similar to the southern Italian dish *zucchine alla scapece*, is a classic of the city's Jewish tradition. The simple preparation of frying vegetables and marinating them in vinegar likely arrived with Sephardic Jews fleeing Spanish dominion in 1492. Of course, there were no squash back then, but Spain claims a similar preparation called escabeche, so there's a good chance the *concia* technique has Spanish roots. Romans use *zucchine romanesche*, a pale-green, fluted variety, but feel free to substitute your local zucchini, other squash, or eggplant. Early in the season, zucchini doesn't require salting, but later on, when the seeds are bigger, we recommend doing so to improve its texture and remove bitterness.

serves 4 to 6 as a side dish or makes 3 to 4 sandwiches

2 garlic cloves, thinly sliced

¼ cup fresh mint or basil leaves, finely chopped, plus more for garnish

⅔ cup white wine vinegar

Neutral oil (see page 27), for frying

6 or 7 zucchini, cut into ¼-inch-thick rounds (6½ cups sliced)

1 teaspoon sea salt

Extra-virgin olive oil, for dressing

Combine the garlic, mint, and vinegar in a medium bowl and set aside.

Line a wire rack with paper towels. In a medium frying pan or cast-iron skillet, heat 2 inches of neutral oil to 350°F. Fry the zucchini in small batches until golden brown or darker, if you wish, and transfer to the rack to drain. Season with the salt.

Add the zucchini to the vinegar marinade and toss to coat. Marinate in the refrigerator for at least 2 hours or overnight.

Serve garnished with additional fresh mint and drizzled with olive oil, on its own as a side dish or as a sandwich filling: Slice open bread such as Passi's *Ciabattina* (page 192), fill with *concia*, and drizzle with some leftover marinade.

If the zucchini are very bitter, salt them in advance. Place the zucchini slices in a colander set over a bowl or over the sink and sprinkle with salt. Allow the slices to sit for an hour or two; some liquid will drain out. Rinse and pat dry before frying.

---

spaghetti con cicoria e bottarga

SPAGHETTI WITH DANDELION GREENS AND CURED FISH ROE

CICORIA is Rome's ubiquitous bitter leafy green. It grows wild all over town, and market stalls are piled high with the weed practically year-round. While *cicoria* has been a perennial favorite for ages, bottarga, cured fish roe, arrived a bit later in the 1960s when Jews escaped to Rome from Libya, bringing their culinary traditions with them. Libyan Jewish housewives began serving savory bottarga grated over strands of spaghetti tossed with sautéed *cicoria*. It has since migrated from homes to restaurants; Nonna Betta in the former Jewish Ghetto does an especially delicious version.

serves 4 to 6

Sea salt

1 pound dandelion greens

3 tablespoons extra-virgin olive oil, plus more to taste

3 garlic cloves, smashed

2 teaspoons *peperoncino* or red pepper flakes

1 pound spaghetti

¼ cup grated Pecorino Romano (optional)

1 (3-inch) piece bottarga

Bring a large pot of water to a rolling boil over high heat. Salt the water. When the salt has dissolved, add the dandelion greens and blanch until tender, about a minute. Transfer to a colander to drain. Allow the dandelion greens to cool, about 10 minutes, then squeeze out any remaining water and coarsely chop the greens. Set aside.

Heat the olive oil in a large skillet over medium heat. When the oil begins to shimmer, add the garlic and cook until just golden, about 5 minutes. Add the *peperoncino* and cook until fragrant, about 30 seconds. Add the dandelion greens and cook until the leaves darken, about 10 minutes.

Meanwhile, bring a large pot of water to a boil over high heat. Salt the water. When the salt has dissolved, add the pasta and cook until al dente (see page 34). Drain and transfer to a large serving bowl. Add the dandelion greens and Pecorino Romano (if using). Toss well, adding additional olive oil if desired.

Divide the pasta among individual plates and grate bottarga to taste over each serving.

hraimi con couscous

SPICY FISH WITH COUSCOUS

HRAIMI, a spicy fish dish, is a Shabbat classic and a pillar of the *cucina tripolina* (see page 119), the cuisine of Rome's Libyan Jews. The *peperoncino*-spiked sauce takes time to penetrate the flesh of the fish, so it's best to cook the dish in advance and allow it to marinate overnight, which would be in typical Shabbat fashion. For optimum flavor, salt the fish 20 minutes before cooking.

serves 4

¼ cup extra-virgin olive oil

2 yellow onions, diced

Sea salt

1 tablespoon hot paprika

1 tablespoon *peperoncino* or red pepper flakes

1 teaspoon ground caraway

1 tablespoon ground cumin

¼ cup tomato paste

1½ tablespoons fresh lemon juice (from ½ lemon)

2 pounds amberjack steaks or sea bass fillets, about 1½ inches thick, salted in advance

3 cups cooked couscous

Heat the olive oil in a medium saucepan over medium-low heat. When the oil begins to shimmer, add the onions. Season with salt and cook, stirring, until translucent and very soft, about 20 minutes. Add the paprika, *peperoncino*, caraway, and cumin. Cook until fragrant, about 1 minute. Add the tomato paste and cook until it turns a deep brick red, about 2 minutes. Add the lemon juice and 1 cup water and stir to incorporate. Simmer over low heat, covered, for 15 to 20 minutes, stirring occasionally.

Carefully lower the fish into the sauce and cook over medium heat until opaque and cooked through, about 15 minutes, or 10 minutes per inch of thickness.

Serve with couscous immediately or the following day.

triglie con cipolle, pinoli, e uvetta

RED MULLET WITH ONIONS, PINE NUTS, AND RAISINS

YOM KIPPUR, the Day of Atonement, is a most solemn holiday for Jews worldwide and particularly for observant communities like that in Rome, where centuries of persecution have amplified the importance of traditions. This dish is the typical Roman Jewish food for breaking the daylong fast that is part of the practice. The pine nuts and raisins, a common combination in Sephardic Jewish cooking, speak to its origins. Salt the fish an hour or so ahead for a more flavorful outcome.

serves 4 to 6

¼ cup extra-virgin olive oil	Preheat the oven to 350°F.
3 yellow onions, thinly sliced	Heat the olive oil in a medium ovenproof skillet over medium heat. When the oil begins to shimmer, add the onions, season with salt, and cook until translucent, about 10 minutes. Add the pine nuts, raisins, vinegar, and ½ cup water. Place the fish on top and bring the liquid to a simmer.
Sea salt	
¼ cup pine nuts, lightly toasted	
⅓ cup raisins	Cover the pan and transfer to the oven. Bake for 10 minutes, then uncover and continue cooking until the fish is cooked through, 5 minutes more. Remove from the oven and serve warm.
¼ cup white wine vinegar	
2 pounds whole red mullet, scaled, cleaned, rinsed, and salted	

scaloppine con lattuga ripiena

VEAL SCALLOPINI WITH STUFFED LETTUCE

LETTUCE, frisée, chard, and dandelion greens all figure heavily in Rome's Jewish cuisine. The same seventeenth-century sumptuary laws that limited the consumption of meat and fish also restricted access to produce, limiting it primarily to wild plants and lettuces. Even today, the community's classics incorporate an abundance of leafy produce as an evergreen reminder of the past. This dish features stuffed lettuce studded with anchovies and olives as a partner to thinly pounded veal.

serves 4

½ cup all-purpose flour

1½ pounds veal scallopini, patted dry and pounded into ⅛-inch thickness

Sea salt and freshly ground black pepper

4 salted anchovy fillets, cleaned (see below) and chopped into ¼-inch pieces

8 black olives, pitted and chopped into ¼-inch pieces

1 large head romaine lettuce, cut into 4 wedges

2 tablespoons extra-virgin olive oil

Put the flour in a shallow medium dish. Season the veal all over with salt and pepper. Dredge each veal cutlet in the flour, shaking off any excess, and set aside.

Mix the anchovies and olives together in a small bowl. Work them into the spaces between the romaine leaves in each wedge. Set aside.

Heat the olive oil in a medium skillet over medium heat. When the oil begins to shimmer, working in batches, add the veal and cook until it shrinks and browns slightly, about 1 minute per side. Transfer to a serving plate and set aside.

Add the stuffed lettuce wedges to the same pan. Season to taste. Cover the pan and cook the lettuce until browned on one side with a slight crunch in the center, about 2 minutes. Drizzle with any oil, anchovies, and olives remaining in the pan. Serve alongside the veal.

When choosing anchovies, we recommend the salt-packed variety over those packed in oil. Their flavor and subtlety are much greater. Salted anchovies are available at Italian specialty stores or via mail order (see Resources, page 249). To clean salted anchovies, rinse them under cold running water and rub gently to loosen the salt and scales. With your fingers, break off the tail fin, then loosen and remove the spine. Rinse well and soak in cold water. After 15 minutes, taste for salt. If the anchovies are extremely salty, repeat the rinsing process until they are just slightly salty.

---

aliciotti con l'indivia

ANCHOVY AND FRISÉE CASSEROLE

AFTER *carciofi alla giudia*, this dish is the most iconic in Roman Jewish cuisine and was a Ghetto staple, likely influenced by the seventeenth-century sumptuary laws that limited the types of fish Rome's Jews were permitted to buy. Brilliant in its humble simplicity, its peasant origins don't mean this casserole lacks flavor or depth. You can top it with fine or coarse bread crumbs if you wish, or omit them altogether, placing the focus on the slightly bitter greens and the flavorful fresh fish.

serves 6 to 8

Sea salt

1 large head frisée (curly endive)

3 tablespoons extra-virgin olive oil

Freshly ground black pepper

1 pound fresh anchovies, cleaned and filleted

½ cup Seasoned Bread Crumbs (page 164; optional)

Preheat the oven to 400°F.

Bring a large pot of water to a rolling boil over high heat. Salt the water. When the salt has dissolved, add the frisée and blanch until tender, about 1 minute. Drain, squeeze, and set aside.

Pour half the olive oil into a round 12-inch baking dish. Layer half the frisée in the bottom of the dish. Season generously with salt and pepper, then cover with half the anchovies, arranging them in a radial pattern. Repeat the frisée and anchovy layers once more. Sprinkle bread crumbs evenly on top, if desired, then drizzle with the remaining olive oil.

Bake for 20 minutes, or until the top is golden. If there is any water in the dish when you remove it from the oven, drain it off. Cut the casserole into wedges and serve warm or at room temperature.

LA CUCINA TRIPOLINA

ON THE MORNING of Monday, June 6, 1967, the Libyan cities of Tripoli and Benghazi erupted in anti-Semitic violence. In the days and weeks that followed, Jewish businesses were destroyed, property was confiscated, and Jews were beaten and even killed. In the midst of the pogroms, the Libyan government scrambled to evacuate its Jewish citizens, issuing exit visas aimed at prohibiting their return. Libyan Jews boarded boats and planes bound for Italy, and by the end of that year, some five thousand had landed on Italian soil. Some were housed in the Roman Jewish neighborhood of Piazza Bologna, while others were sent to refugee camps south of Rome. Although there are no official statistics, an estimated 1,500 to 1,800 stayed, while others immigrated to Israel. Today some 4,500 Libyan Jews live in Rome, this religious and ethnic minority accounting for about a third of the city's Jewish community.

As for any Jews living in the diaspora, family networks and religious identity are essential to Libyan Jews. Eating Libyan food was, and continues to be, an important expression of cultural identity. Among first-generation Libyan Jews, eating the *cucina tripolina* is a daily occurrence. The unique cuisine, named after the Libyan capital of Tripoli, consists of dishes rooted in the flavors and preparations of North Africa. Stews enriched with spices like cinnamon, cumin, caraway, paprika, and turmeric are common. Garlic, peppers, onion, kosher meat, and fish are all major protagonists.

Many of the restaurateurs, butchers, and kosher food shop owners in the historic Jewish Ghetto, as well as Piazza Bologna, are of Libyan origin, allowing them to preserve and pass on traditions. Typical dishes include *Hraimi con Couscous* (page 113), *mafrum* (stuffed vegetables), *shakshuka* (eggs in a spicy tomato sauce), *lubya b'selk* (beans with spinach), *taershi* (a garlic-rich pumpkin spread), and *brik*. *Ajij*, similar to *Pizzarelle* (page 124), cookies, and phyllo pastries are sweetened with honey or syrup and flavored with dried fruits, nuts, and sesame seeds. Each intensely flavored, liberally spiced specialty is both a connection to and a reminder of a lost homeland.

brodo di pesce

FISH SOUP

THE PORTICO D'OTTAVIA, brick and marble ruins on the edge of the former Ghetto, hosted a fish market for about eight centuries. During the Ghetto era, it was a major source of food for the neighboring Jews. They lived off small fish and fish scraps, simmering them with vegetables to create flavorful broths. Although the market and Ghetto are long gone, the Portico d'Ottavia still stands, as does the legacy of this peasant dish. The local community continues the tradition of simmering fish belonging to a category called *pesce azzuro*, so-called blue fish—oily fish from the nearby sea, including mackerel, sardines, and anchovies—serving it with the comforting, enriched broth in which it cooks.

serves 4 to 6

¼ cup plus 2 tablespoons extra-virgin olive oil

2 carrots, diced

2 celery stalks, diced

1 yellow onion, diced

2 garlic cloves, smashed

1 teaspoon sea salt

1 (28-ounce) can tomato puree

Leaves from 6 sprigs fresh flat-leaf parsley, chopped

1½ pounds mackerel, sardine, or anchovy fillets, cleaned and scaled

Heat the olive oil in a large pot over medium-low heat. When the oil begins to shimmer, add the carrots, celery, onion, and garlic. Cook until the onion is translucent and all the ingredients are soft, about 15 minutes. Season with the salt, then add the tomato puree and parsley.

Bring to a simmer, then add the fish fillets and simmer over low heat until the fish is opaque and cooked through.

Remove the pan from the heat and, if desired, pass everything through a food mill to achieve a chunky, thick soup. Season to taste and serve immediately.

polpette di pollo in bianco

CHICKEN MEATBALLS IN WHITE WINE SAUCE

PEASANT CUISINES don't waste anything, and especially not stale bread. Rome's *cucina ebraica* relied on it as filler for meatballs throughout the Ghetto period. Now, the proportion of bread has shifted to favor meat, which is more easily accessible. This dish merges an old Ghetto recipe with inspiration from the *cucina tripolina* (see page 119) in the form of spices and pistachios. The meatballs are made with a white wine–based sauce instead of tomato, which allows the flavors of the dish to shine through.

makes 30 to 35 **polpette**

3 slices day-old bread of any kind, crusts removed

1 cup chicken broth or water plus more for cooking, warmed

1¾ pounds ground chicken

2 large eggs, lightly beaten

1 garlic clove, minced

1 teaspoon sea salt, plus more as needed

Freshly ground black pepper

½ teaspoon ground cinnamon

¼ teaspoon freshly grated nutmeg

3 tablespoons pistachios, chopped

2 packed tablespoons fresh flat-leaf parsley, finely chopped

¼ cup plus 2 tablespoons extra-virgin olive oil

2 medium shallots, minced

½ cup all-purpose flour

½ cup dry white wine

1½ tablespoons fresh lemon juice (from ½ lemon)

Soak the bread for a few minutes in 1 cup warm chicken broth. When it has softened, squeeze out the excess liquid and place the bread in a large bowl.

Add the ground chicken, eggs, garlic, salt, pepper to taste, cinnamon, nutmeg, pistachios, and half the parsley. Mix thoroughly by hand. Form the mixture into balls roughly the size of walnuts and set aside.

In a large frying pan or cast-iron skillet, heat the olive oil over medium heat. When the oil begins to shimmer, add the shallots and a pinch of salt and cook until soft, about 5 minutes. Meanwhile, lightly dust the meatballs all over with flour (a mesh strainer works well for this) and shake off any excess. Add them to the pan and brown all over. Add the wine, scraping up any browned bits from the sides and bottom of the pan with a wooden spoon or heatproof spatula. When the alcohol aroma dissipates, about a minute, add enough broth or water to cover the meatballs about halfway. Bring to a simmer, reduce the heat to low, and cook, covered, until a creamy sauce has formed, 10 to 15 minutes, stirring occasionally.

Season with lemon juice, garnish with the remaining parsley, and serve the meatballs warm or at room temperature with sauce spooned over.

If the meatball mixture is sticky, wet your hands with warm water before rolling.

pizzarelle

HONEY-SOAKED MATZO FRITTERS

A FEW DAYS a year, Boccione "Il Forno del Ghetto," the generations-old kosher bakery on Via Portico d'Ottavia, sells *pizzarelle*. The bakers make them only during Passover, and due to restrictions on working, the bakery is closed during most of the holiday. If you time it right, this highly seasonal specialty can be yours. Otherwise, drop by Boccione for their year-round non-Passover classics like thick ricotta cakes and *Biscotti con Mandorle e Cannella* (page 126). And don't be turned off by the slightly charred tops of, well, everything they sell. It's the trademark of this well-loved institution. In case you do miss it, though, this recipe is an excellent substitution for their *pizzarelle*.

makes 20 to 24 pizzarelle

4 sheets matzo

1 large egg, separated

5 tablespoons sugar

½ cup pine nuts

⅓ cup raisins

1½ teaspoons orange zest

Pinch of sea salt

Neutral oil (see page 27), for frying

Honey, for serving

Break the matzo into large pieces and place them in a medium bowl. Pour over about 1½ cups water, being sure that the edges of the matzo are covered. Soak the pieces for 15 minutes, turning them every 5 minutes, until soft and damp and no hard bits remain.

Drain and squeeze any excess water out of the matzo and transfer to a separate medium bowl. Add the egg yolk, sugar, pine nuts, raisins, orange zest, and salt and mix well. In a separate medium bowl, beat the egg white to stiff peaks. Gently fold the egg white into the matzo mixture until no streaks remain, taking care not to deflate.

In a small skillet, heat 2 inches of neutral oil to 350°F. Using two spoons or a small ice cream scoop, carefully drop small rounds of the batter into the hot oil. Fry in batches for 5 minutes or until golden brown, turning once to ensure even cooking.

Drain on paper towels for a few minutes, then transfer to a plate and drizzle with honey before serving.

frittata di zucca

PUMPKIN FRITTATA

ALL OVER the world during Rosh Hashanah, families gather to celebrate the Jewish New Year. The ritual meal for the holiday is meant to be rich with symbolic foods including apples, pomegranates, beets, and gourds. The gourd of choice for Rome's Sephardic Jews is the locally cultivated pumpkin, which wards off evil and signifies aspirations for a trouble-free year ahead. Here, the symbolic pumpkin is paired with eggs, an ingredient particularly prominent in the Roman Jewish tradition. They feature heavily in the *cucina ebraica* because they are *parve*, or neutral, and therefore can be consumed at any kosher meal, whether meat or dairy based.

makes 1 frittata, to serve 4 to 6

¼ cup extra-virgin olive oil

2 medium red onions, thinly sliced

¼ teaspoon sea salt, plus more as needed

1 pound pumpkin, butternut squash, or other winter squash, peeled, seeded, and cut into ½-inch cubes

2 medium potatoes, peeled and cut into ½-inch cubes

1 tablespoon chopped fresh sage

¼ teaspoon ground cinnamon

8 large eggs

Freshly ground black pepper

Baking the frittata in the oven ensures more even cooking.

Preheat the oven to 325°F.

Heat the olive oil in a large ovenproof skillet over low heat. When the oil begins to shimmer, add the onions. Season with a pinch of salt and cook until softened and translucent, about 10 minutes. Add the pumpkin, potatoes, sage, cinnamon, and another pinch of salt. Increase the heat to medium and continue to cook, stirring, until the vegetables are tender and cooked through, about 15 minutes. If the vegetables start to stick to the bottom, add a few tablespoons of water; aim for a soft, moist vegetable base without too much browning.

Meanwhile, whisk the eggs in a large bowl with salt and pepper to taste. When the vegetables are tender, add the egg mixture to the skillet. Using a wooden spoon, stir a few times, moving from the outside of the pan toward the middle. Once the eggs begin to set around the edge of the pan, about a minute, turn off the heat and transfer the pan to the oven. Bake the frittata for 10 to 15 minutes, or until the edges start to come away from the sides of the pan.

Remove the pan from the oven and allow the frittata to cool before unmolding, about 30 minutes. To unmold, run a heatproof spatula around the edges and underneath the frittata. Slide it onto a serving plate. Serve at room temperature, sliced into wedges.

biscotti con mandorle e cannella

ALMOND AND CINNAMON BISCOTTI

BISCOTTI are made all over Italy but this recipe is unique to the Roman Jewish tradition. Our version is inspired by Boccione "Il Forno del Ghetto," where they are sold by endearingly grumpy ladies in their crowded, spartan bakery.

makes 36 biscotti

2 cups whole raw almonds

2¾ cups all-purpose flour, plus more for dusting

1¼ cups sugar

½ teaspoon sea salt

1½ tablespoons ground cinnamon

1½ teaspoons baking powder

3 large eggs

3 large egg yolks

2 teaspoons pure vanilla extract

1 teaspoon orange zest

1 tablespoon whole milk

Preheat the oven to 350°F. Place the almonds on a parchment paper–lined baking sheet and bake for 10 minutes. Remove from the oven and allow to cool until they can be handled, about 20 minutes. Leave the oven on and set the lined baking sheet aside.

In a large bowl, whisk together the flour, sugar, salt, cinnamon, and baking powder. In a separate medium bowl, whisk together the eggs, two of the egg yolks, the vanilla, and the orange zest.

Add the cooled almonds to the flour mixture, then pour in the egg mixture. Mix with a spoon until the dough comes together, then knead until the almonds are evenly distributed.

Turn the dough out onto a lightly floured surface and divide it into two equal pieces. Roll each piece into a log about 1½ inches in diameter. Place the logs on the lined baking sheet with at least 2 inches between them. Gently press to flatten the logs to a height of 1 inch.

In a small bowl, whisk together the remaining egg yolk with the milk. Brush the logs with the egg wash.

Bake the logs for 30 minutes. Remove from the oven and allow to cool until they can be handled, about 30 minutes, then cut into approximately ½-inch slices (about eighteen pieces). Return the slices to the lined baking sheet and bake for 15 minutes more, until the cookies are no longer soft when pressed.

Remove from the oven and allow the biscotti to cool for 10 minutes on the baking sheet, then transfer to a wire rack. They will keep in a sealed container for up to 10 days.

QUINTO QUARTO

When the slaughterhouse operated in Testaccio (see page 132) from the 1880s to 1975, butchers divided animals into prestigious cuts for nobles, bureaucrats, and soldiers. Butchers, slaughterhouse workers, and lower-class Romans ate the remaining off-cuts and organs, or *quinto quarto* ("fifth quarter"), so-called because they accounted for one-quarter of the animal's weight. Offal may not be quite as popular as it used to be, but those recipes invented in the simple taverns around the slaughterhouse are still served on restaurant and home tables today.

fettuccine con rigaglie di pollo

FETTUCINE WITH CHICKEN INNARDS RAGÙ

FRESH PASTA and a hearty chicken innards ragù were once a classic combination in Rome's countryside. Farmers and vineyard workers would enjoy a full poultry-centric lunch, beginning with egg-based pasta bathed in a tomato sauce enriched by chicken hearts, livers, and gizzards, followed by *Pollo alla Romana* (page 89), chicken cooked with tomatoes and bell peppers. Rural life may be in decline, but city dwellers still enjoy this dish, mainly at restaurants, in the hot summer months. If you can't find chicken gizzards or hearts, the recipe works well with just the livers.

serves 4 to 6

Sea salt

4 ounces chicken gizzards, cleaned

2 tablespoons extra-virgin olive oil

1 onion, diced

1 carrot, diced

1 celery stalk, diced

4 ounces chicken hearts, chopped

1 cup white wine

1 (14-ounce) can crushed tomatoes

4 ounces chicken livers, chopped

1 pound fettuccine

½ cup grated Pecorino Romano

Bring a medium pot of water to a very gentle simmer over low heat. Salt the water. When the salt has dissolved, add the gizzards and poach them over low heat until tender, about 2 hours. Drain, cool, and chop the gizzards into ¼-inch pieces.

Heat the olive oil in a large pan over medium-low heat. When the oil begins to shimmer, add the onion, carrot, celery, and a pinch of salt and cook until the vegetables have softened, about 15 minutes. Add the chicken hearts and sauté for a few minutes until they change color. Add the white wine and cook until the alcohol aroma dissipates, about a minute. Add the tomatoes and simmer for 30 minutes over low heat, until thickened, then add the livers and gizzards, using a spoon to break them apart if they stick together. Cook for 1 minute, until the livers are cooked through but not chalky.

While the tomato sauce cooks, bring a large pot of water to a rolling boil over high heat. Salt the water. When the salt has dissolved, add the pasta and cook until it is al dente (see page 34).

Drain the fettuccine, reserving the pasta cooking water, and add the pasta to the sauce, mixing well to coat. Adjust the consistency of the sauce with pasta cooking water if necessary. Season to taste.

Plate and sprinkle each portion with Pecorino Romano.

To prevent overcooking the chicken innards, add them to the pan when the pasta is al dente.

TESTACCIO

NO NEIGHBORHOOD in Rome's historical center preserves
such a distinct character as Testaccio. The area's unique atmosphere
developed, in part, due to its relative isolation; two sides are trimmed
by a dramatic curve in the Tiber River. The third-century Aurelian
Walls and the lower slopes of the Aventine Hill define Testaccio's
remaining borders. Unlike Rome's other central zones, most of Testaccio
was developed with an urban plan in mind. The rectangular piazzas
and gridlike street plan were imposed on what was a fairly sparse
palette when the area was built for industrial use and public housing in
the late nineteenth and early twentieth centuries.

Testaccio's history goes back much further; for two thousand years
the area has been linked to food and commerce. During antiquity,
polychrome stones arrived on Testaccio's banks from Turkey, Tunisia,
and Greece, while olive oil and wine came mainly from Spain and
North Africa. This ancient commerce is visible in the excavated ruins
beside Ponte Sublicio, the bridge linking Testaccio to Trastevere. But
the greatest testament to Testaccio's role in Roman trade is the zone's
distinct topographical feature, Monte dei Cocci, also known as Monte di
Testaccio. The man-made hill, more than half a mile in circumference
and rising 115 feet high, is composed of tens of millions of terra-cotta
amphorae, kiln-baked clay jugs used to transport olive oil to Rome,
mainly in the second to fourth centuries. These vessels were heaped
into a pile because they were either broken or unsuitable for further
use. Today, they are the symbol of modern Testaccio.

In the fourth century, Rome's commercial activities began to
decline and Testaccio fell into a state of abandonment. For more
than one thousand years, the hill and Testaccio in general remained
suburban, sparsely populated zones. Shepherds grazed their flocks
and burrowed grottoes into the hillside for shelter. But, for the most
part, nature overwhelmed the ruins, giving root to hundreds of species
of plants, many of which are still visible today. During the Middle
Ages, Testaccio's idyllic setting was used for Carnival games. In the
Renaissance, the peak of Monte di Testaccio became the destination of
the *Via Crucis* on Good Friday. In the eighteenth century, Testaccio was
the site of the *Ottobrate Romane*, an autumn harvest festival.

The defining moment in Testaccio's contemporary history was the inauguration of the city's slaughterhouse on the banks of the Tiber River in 1887. The sprawling complex was laid out over a million-square-foot area between Monte dei Cocci and the Tiber River. The massive pavilions where the animals were slaughtered, skinned, and broken down still survive, though slaughter activity ceased in 1975. Historic *osterie* and butchers continue to thrive in Testaccio and specialize in *quinto quarto*.

Today, restaurants like Checchino dal 1887 and Flavio al Velavevodetto, both built into Monte dei Cocci, cater to a well-heeled clientele hungry for Testaccio's *quinto quarto* classics like tripe, oxtail, intestines, trotters, and brains. Nearby, in the Nuovo Mercato di Testaccio, inaugurated in 2012, butcher shops like Macelleria Sartor specialize in offal, while Mordi e Vai serves sandwiches made from simmered organs and poor cuts. The slaughterhouse itself has been repurposed. One branch of the University of Rome's architecture department and a retiree social club occupy adjacent areas. A museum for contemporary art (MACRO), which hosts art installations and exhibitions, sprawls over an enormous area, encompassing former courtyards and pavilions. Another area houses a refugee camp, and beside that, the Città dell'Altra Economia promotes organic food commerce at its café, supermarket, and Sunday farmers' market. Clearly, Testaccio was born out of food commerce, and it remains close to those origins today.

animelle con marsala

SWEETBREADS WITH MARSALA WINE

SWEETBREADS are the thymus glands of veal and lambs, which disappear when the animal reaches maturity. Like the young animals from which they come, they are tender and delicate when cooked right. This creamy preparation is spiked with a splash of Marsala, a wine from the western coast of Sicily. In spite of its distant production, the fortified wine is at home in Rome, where it has been featured in sweet and savory dishes for well over a century. Before you begin cooking, soak the sweetbreads briefly in water, changing it several times, until the blood and impurities are removed and the water runs clean. There's no need to soak them in milk—that's an old wives' tale.

serves 4 to 6

Sea salt

1 pound veal sweetbreads, soaked

Freshly ground black pepper

All-purpose flour, for dredging

3 tablespoons salted butter

¾ cup Marsala wine

1 tablespoon fresh lemon juice

Fill a large bowl with ice and water. Bring a large pot of water to a gentle simmer over low heat. Salt the water. When the salt has dissolved, add the sweetbreads and poach for 5 minutes, then transfer to the ice water bath to stop the cooking and cool.

Once the sweetbreads have cooled, about 5 minutes, break the lobes into large pieces, and peel off and discard the thin membrane that encases each piece. Pat dry with a paper towel. Season them with salt and pepper to taste, then dredge in flour, shaking off any excess.

Melt the butter in a large skillet over medium heat. Once the butter foams and then subsides, add the sweetbreads. Sear for about 3 minutes on each side, until golden brown. Remove and set aside. Add the Marsala to the pan and scrape up any brown bits from the bottom. Boil and reduce the Marsala until the alcohol has evaporated and the sauce has thickened, 1 to 2 minutes, then add the lemon juice.

Serve the sweetbreads immediately with the pan sauce drizzled over.

fegatelli di maiale

GRILLED PIG'S LIVER

BAY LEAVES, caul fat, pig's liver, seasoning, vinegar, and heat are all you need to make this stunningly simple and satisfying dish. Once a common delicacy eaten immediately after the winter pig slaughters, pork livers are now harder to come by. The caul fat holds the bay leaf to the surface of the liver, aromatizing the liver as it cooks.

serves 4

1 pound pork liver, cut into 4 rectangular pieces

Kosher salt and freshly ground black pepper

5 ounces caul fat, cut into 4 pieces of about 4 × 4 inches each

¼ cup white wine vinegar

4 fresh bay leaves

Neutral oil (see page 27), for frying

Generously season the pork liver pieces with salt and pepper. Set aside for 30 minutes to 1 hour.

Meanwhile, in a medium bowl, soak the caul fat in warm water to cover along with the vinegar until softened, 20 to 30 minutes. Remove and pat dry.

Spread a piece of the caul fat out on a clean, dry work surface. Place a piece of liver in the center and place 1 bay leaf on top. Wrap the fat around to create a parcel. Pat the outside dry with a paper towel. Repeat to make four caul-wrapped liver parcels.

Heat a medium grill pan or a medium oiled skillet over high heat. When the pan is smoking hot or the oil begins to shimmer, add the liver and cook until it is just cooked through, about 4 minutes per side. The liver should still be rosy in the center.

Remove the livers from the heat and allow them to rest for 2 to 3 minutes, then serve. You can eat the caul fat, but remove the bay leaves as you eat.

lingua in salsa verde

BEEF TONGUE IN SALSA VERDE

IN ROME, tongues are sold whole from butcher's stalls, then simmered and served with *Salsa Verde*, a garlic-rich parsley sauce typical of Piedmontese cooking. When a king from Piedmont unified Italy in 1870, thousands of northerners converged on the newly appointed Italian capital, bringing their tangy condiments and securing a place for them in Roman cuisine. Begin this recipe by coating the tongue in kosher salt, then refrigerate for at least 24 hours before cooking.

serves 4 to 6

1 whole beef tongue (2 pounds), salted in advance

1 carrot

1 celery stalk

1 yellow onion

1 bay leaf

3 to 4 whole cloves

1 cup dry white wine

Salsa Verde **(recipe follows), for serving**

Place the salted tongue in a large pot. Cover with cold water and bring to a gentle simmer over low heat, skimming off any foam that rises to the top. Add the carrot, celery, onion, bay leaf, cloves, and wine and continue to simmer until the tongue is fork-tender and the skin easily separates from the muscle, 2 to 3 hours. Turn off the heat and allow the tongue to cool in the cooking liquid.

Remove the tongue from the pot. Peel off the skin, trim any visible veins, and cut crosswise into ¼-inch-thick slices. Serve at room temperature with *Salsa Verde* alongside.

salsa verde

makes 1½ cups

1 cup coarsely torn soft bread crumbs

2 tablespoons white wine vinegar

Leaves from 2 bunches fresh flat-leaf parsley, chopped

1 salted anchovy, cleaned and filleted (see page 116), then chopped

1 tablespoon capers, chopped

½ cup extra-virgin olive oil

In a medium bowl, combine the bread and vinegar and set aside until the vinegar has been fully absorbed, about 10 minutes. Add the parsley, anchovy, and capers. Add olive oil slowly, stirring well to incorporate.

Serve also with *Polpette di Bollito* (page 52) or *Insalata di Nervetti* (page 141).

FRINGE FOODS

ROMANS are borderline addicted to their city's classic dishes. But that doesn't mean they have the same voracity for all of them as they used to. Chalk it up to an evolving food culture, changing palates, and new hygiene laws, but a huge range of foods and ingredients that were once central to the Roman diet have faded to the fringes.

Take eels from the Tiber, for example. Romans consumed fresh catch from their river for thousands of years, but plummeting demand and concerns over pollution have destroyed the local fishing industry. Brothers Cesare and Alfredo Bergamini are the last eel fishermen left. Laws prohibit them from selling live eels, so their catch ends up in Naples, where enforcement of such laws is looser.

In 1992, selling pig's blood, an important by-product of the winter slaughter season, was banned, ending a centuries-old tradition. Perishable innards and blood were the first parts to be consumed after an animal was killed; these items formed the basis of great feasts. Pig's blood was even used in desserts, imparting a distinct flavor and texture.

In the wake of mad cow disease, veal brains and *pajata* (intestines) were banned in 2001. The cooked intestines of milk-fed veal were a beloved delicacy to some Romans, so a small black market emerged. A few restaurants and butchers sold *pajata* illegally, while others respected the legislation and used lamb intestines as a substitute. The ban on veal *pajata* was finally lifted in 2015, returning veal intestines to those who crave the flavors and textures most diners have banished to the fringe.

insalata di nervetti

BOILED VEAL CARTILAGE AND TENDONS

NERVETTI are the cartilage of beef and veal knees and the tendons from the shanks. In order to break down the collagen and elastin that make the *nervetti* tough, they need to be simmered for a long time. The results are still chewy, but it's a meal that no poor table would have turned away. The classic Roman preparation calls for tossing bits of *nervetti* with carrots, celery, beans, and a bit of *Salsa Verde*. They are served as a starter.

serves 4 to 6 as a starter

FOR THE NERVETTI

5 pounds veal knees and shanks with tendon attached, washed under cold water

2 bay leaves

¾ cup white wine vinegar

10 whole black peppercorns

3 tablespoons sea salt

8 sprigs fresh flat-leaf parsley, picked

FOR THE SALAD

2 cups *borlotti* (cranberry beans), cooked

Leaves from 8 sprigs fresh flat-leaf parsley, chopped

1 carrot, halved lengthwise and thinly sliced

1 celery stalk, thinly sliced

Sea salt and freshly ground black pepper

Lemon juice

¼ cup *Salsa Verde* (page 139)

Make the *nervetti*: Place the knees and shanks in large pot and add cold water to cover. Bring to a slow simmer over low heat, then add the bay leaves, vinegar, peppercorns, salt, and parsley stems. Simmer for 2 to 3 hours, until the tendons have softened and begin to pull away from the bones. Remove them from the water and allow to cool on the countertop until they can be handled, 20 to 30 minutes. Pull the *nervetti* away from the bones, discarding the bones, and cut into 1-inch pieces.

Make the salad: In a large bowl, combine the *nervetti*, beans, parsley leaves, carrot, celery, salt, pepper, and lemon juice to taste. Toss with the *Salsa Verde*, season to taste, and serve immediately.

In the absence of fresh *borlotti,* feel free to substitute canned.

trippa alla romana

TRIPE WITH TOMATO SAUCE, MINT, AND PECORINO

RENAISSANCE COOKBOOKS name a number of methods for cooking beef tripe, the upper stomachs of grazing cows. But in modern Rome, it is prepared by one method only: honeycomb tripe, called *cuffia* locally, is simmered with tomato and *menta romana*, a variety of local mint. *Trippa alla Romana* is so entrenched in the local cuisine that, unlike many other classic dishes, its elements almost never waver. Book tripe, called *centopelli*, is rarely used. Roman chefs declare it cat food, a possible dig at Florentines, who prefer it to other tripe forms.

serves 4 to 6

2 pounds honeycomb tripe, washed

¼ cup sea salt, plus more as needed

3 tablespoons extra-virgin olive oil

1 medium yellow onion, coarsely chopped

1 carrot, chopped

1 cup white wine

1 (14-ounce) can crushed tomatoes

Leaves from 4 sprigs fresh mint, chopped

1½ cups grated Pecorino Romano

Place the tripe in a large pot and add cold water to cover. Bring to a boil over high heat. Drain and repeat. Drain again. Return the tripe to the pot and again add cold water to cover. Bring to a boil over medium-low heat. Add the salt and simmer until the tripe is fork-tender, about 3 hours. Drain, rinse under cold water, then cut the tripe into ½-inch strips.

Heat the olive oil in a large pan over medium-low heat. When the oil begins to shimmer, add the onion and carrot. Season with a pinch of salt. Cook, stirring, until the onion and carrot are softened, about 15 minutes. Add the wine and cook until the alcohol aroma dissipates, about 1 minute. Add the tomatoes and the sliced tripe and cook for about 1 hour. Turn off the heat, add the mint and 1 cup of Pecorino Romano, and mix well. Season to taste.

Plate and sprinkle each portion with the remaining Pecorino Romano. Serve immediately.

Menta romana (*Mentha pulegium*), a subtly sweet variety of mint, pairs extraordinarily well with the flavors of dishes like *trippa alla romana*. Also common is *mentuccia* (*Calamintha nepeta*), which you're likely to find wedged into the leaves of artichokes before being simmered. In fact, marketgoers are given a complimentary fistful of this mint-like herb with each artichoke purchase. While *menta romana* is hard to come by outside of Rome, *mentuccia*, which goes by lesser calamint and nepitella, can be found in the United States.

simmenthal di coda

OXTAIL TERRINE

DESPITE ITALY'S reputation as a country that supports small producers and embraces organic foods, mass-produced foods have a fairly secure place in the national consciousness (Nutella, anyone?). Visit any deli or supermarket for proof; the majority of foods sold at such venues come from large factories rather than tiny farms. Among the oldest Italian industrial products is Simmenthal, canned boiled beef similar to Spam, which, despite the hideous suction noise it makes as it exits the can, is actually quite delicious. At Mazzo in eastern Rome's Centocelle neighborhood, chefs Francesca Barreca and Marco Baccanelli make their own version of Simmenthal using oxtails, a common Roman ingredient. We have adapted their individual portions to make a terrine. For best results, salt the oxtail with kosher salt 24 hours in advance, allow the cooked oxtail to marinate in its juices overnight, and allow the finished terrine to rest before serving. You'll need some room in your refrigerator—and on your calendar—to make this dish, but it's worth it!

makes one 1-pound terrine

FOR THE OXTAIL

3 tablespoons extra-virgin olive oil

5 pounds salted oxtails

3 carrots, coarsely chopped

2 celery stalks, coarsely chopped

2 small onions, coarsely chopped

4 sprigs fresh thyme

2 bay leaves

10 whole black peppercorns

1 (750 milliliter) bottle dry red wine

6 cups beef or veal broth

Make the oxtail: Heat the olive oil in a large pot over medium-high heat. When the oil begins to shimmer, add the oxtails and cook until browned all over, 10 minutes. Remove from the pot and set aside. Add the carrots, celery, onions, thyme, bay leaves, and peppercorns to the same pot. Sauté until the vegetables are lightly browned, about 15 minutes. Add the wine and scrape up any browned bits from the bottom of the pot. Cook until the alcohol aroma dissipates, about 5 minutes, then return the oxtails to the pot.

Add the broth. Reduce the heat to low and simmer, occasionally skimming off any foam that rises to the top, for about 3 hours, or until the meat is falling off the bone. Remove the pot from the heat, allow to cool for about 1 hour, then refrigerate the meat in the broth overnight.

The next day, skim and discard the fat from the top of the broth. Return the pot to the stovetop over medium-low heat to liquefy the congealed broth. Strain the broth, removing the oxtails and setting them aside, and discard the vegetables and herbs. Pick the meat from the oxtails. Discard the bones, reserving the meat and the broth.

FOR THE TERRINE
FILLING

Sea salt

1 carrot, quartered lengthwise

1 celery stalk, quartered lengthwise

1 bunch fresh flat-leaf parsley, chopped

FOR THE SALAD
(OPTIONAL)

2 fennel bulbs, thinly sliced, fronds reserved

3 celery stalks, leaves on, cut into ¼-inch pieces

1 tablespoon chopped fresh chives

2 or 3 lemons, cut into wedges

FOR THE GARNISH

Freshly ground black pepper

1 bunch fresh flat-leaf parsley leaves, chopped

1 teaspoon lemon zest

Make the terrine filling: Bring a medium pot of water to a boil over high heat. Salt the water. When the salt has dissolved, add the carrot and celery and cook until tender, about 10 minutes.

Line a 1-pound terrine mold or 9 × 5-inch loaf pan with enough plastic wrap to fold over the top, and pack in half the meat. Top with a layer of the boiled carrots and celery and the parsley, distributing it evenly to form a second layer. Pack in the remaining meat to make a third layer. Pour over the reserved broth, which will congeal to hold the meat and vegetables together. Fold the plastic wrap over the top and weigh down the terrine using a smaller mold of the same shape filled with water or another heavy object. Chill it for at least 1 day and up to 3 days before serving. A well-wrapped mold will keep for about a week in the refrigerator.

To unmold the terrine, lift it out of the mold slowly using the plastic wrap and invert it onto a platter. Serve two slices on a bed of sliced fennel, fennel fronds, celery, celery leaves, and chives. Dress with a lemon wedge, or skip the salad and season the terrine with freshly ground pepper, chopped parsley, and grated lemon zest.

You can use the leftover broth from *Polpette di Bollito* (page 52) or *Picchiapò* (page 84).

coda alla vaccinara

BRAISED OXTAIL

NEVER WEAR a white shirt while eating *coda alla vaccinara*—it's a messy one. Oxtail segments are simmered in a tomato sauce for hours until the meat practically falls off the bone. The brick-red sauce, flavored with celery, pine nuts, raisins, and cacao, inevitably drips and splatters when you eat this *quinto quarto* classic the right way: with your hands. Begin this recipe a day in advance—salting the meat with kosher salt 24 hours before cooking to allow the seasoning to penetrate—and, if possible, allow the stew to rest overnight in the refrigerator so its flavors marry and intensify.

serves 4 to 6

2½ ounces *lardo* (cured fatback), or 3 tablespoons olive oil

3½ pounds oxtail, cut into 3-inch segments

1 yellow onion, chopped

1 garlic clove, smashed

5 to 6 whole cloves

2 tablespoons tomato paste

1 cup red wine

1 (28-ounce) can whole peeled tomatoes

Up to 6 cups beef broth (see tip, page 145)

2 celery stalks, cut into 3-inch pieces

¼ cup raisins

¼ cup pine nuts

1 tablespoon cacao or unsweetened cocoa powder

Render the *lardo* in a large pot over medium-high heat, or heat the olive oil until it is shimmering. Add the oxtail segments and cook until browned all over, then remove from the pot and set aside. Reduce the heat to medium-low and add the onion, garlic, and cloves. Cook until the onion is translucent and the garlic has just turned golden, about 10 minutes. Add the tomato paste and cook until it turns a deep brick red, about 5 minutes. Add the wine, scraping up any browned bits from the bottom of the pan, and cook until the alcohol aroma dissipates, about a minute, then add the tomatoes.

Return the meat to the pot and cover three-quarters of the way with the beef broth. Cover and cook until the meat is just falling off the bone, 5 to 6 hours, adding more broth if the sauce reduces too much.

Toward the end of cooking, add the celery, raisins, pine nuts, and cacao, mixing well. Simmer for 20 to 30 minutes more.

Turn off the heat and allow the oxtail to rest for at least 30 minutes, ideally overnight, in the refrigerator. Serve on its own. Use any leftover sauce to dress *Gnocchi di Patate* (page 95).

VERDURE

Rome might seem like a carnivorous cobblestoned city, but the local cuisine is rooted in seasonal produce. The *contorni* (vegetable side dishes) may be tucked at the back of the menu at a restaurant, but they're no afterthought; cooked vegetable sides and, increasingly, salads are a fundamental part of a Roman meal—an opportunity to showcase the city's fresh flavors and produce.

sformatino di broccolo romanesco

ROMANESCO CUSTARD

THE WORD *sformatino* comes from *sformare*, meaning "to unmold," and before serving these soufflé-like savory custards, that's exactly what you'll do. *Sformatini* are popular at Rome's neo-trattorias—those casual eateries that attempt to tweak tradition a bit without alienating the locals. In this recipe, we use *broccolo romanesco* (romanesco in English and just *broccolo* to Romans), which starts showing up on market stalls in late fall.

makes 8 sformatini

Neutral oil (see page 27), for greasing ramekins

3 tablespoons extra-virgin olive oil

1 large yellow onion, sliced

1 pound romanesco, steamed until soft, then chopped

¼ cup white wine

4 large eggs

1½ cups heavy cream

¼ cup grated Pecorino Romano

The ramekins should fit tightly in the roasting pan. If they don't, place a folded dish towel underneath and bake on top of the towel. The water will keep them from scorching.

Preheat the oven to 320°F.

Oil eight 6-ounce ramekins and set them in a roasting pan.

Bring a full kettle of water to a boil over high heat.

While the water boils, heat the olive oil in a medium skillet over medium-low heat. When the oil begins to shimmer, add the onion and cook until just softened, about 8 minutes. Add the romanesco, pour in the wine, and stir with a wooden spoon, breaking up the romanesco with the back of the spoon. Allow the alcohol aroma to dissipate, about a minute, then cook for 5 minutes more.

Transfer the romanesco-onion mixture to a food processor and pulse until smooth. Pass the mixture through a sieve set over a bowl, discarding any solids.

In a large bowl, whisk the eggs, then add the cream. Whisk the romanesco puree into the egg mixture, then add the Pecorino Romano. Ladle the mixture into the prepared ramekins, leaving about ¼ inch of space at the top.

Set the roasting pan on the oven rack and pour the boiling water around the ramekins until the water comes halfway up their sides. Bake for 40 to 45 minutes, until the custard is still a bit wobbly but a knife inserted in the center comes out clean.

Carefully remove the roasting pan from the oven and allow the custards to sit in the water for 10 minutes more before removing them, then let cool.

To serve, carefully unmold onto a small plate.

FORAGING ROME

THE FLAVORS and aromas of Roman cooking are all around us. Even the densest, most urban parts of town bear signs of the city's wild flora, spontaneous plants popping up in surprising places. In the spring, *mentuccia*, *menta romana*, and other minty herbs (see page 142) grow at the base of sun-drenched brick walls, while arugula and dandelion greens form a lush blanket over the Circus Maximus and Roman Forum. Around Easter, the electric-blue flowers of the fuzzy borage plant bloom in roadside ditches and nettles line sidewalks and curbs. Then cascading caper bushes arrive. The plants cling to porous walls, ancient and modern, most notably the Aurelian Walls, Rome's third-century defensive circuit. The springtime buds open and flower, revealing pinkish-white petals. In the summer and fall, succulent purslane plants peek out of sidewalk cracks. Year-round, bay laurel hedges trim tram tracks, noble properties, and public parks, leaves ready for the plucking. Today, these plants may be Weedwacked, uprooted, or crushed underfoot, but their continued presence is a reminder of the bitter, herbal, and vegetal flavors that have informed Roman cooking for centuries.

Toast the hazelnuts on a parchment paper–lined baking sheet in a preheated 280°F oven for about 10 minutes.

insalata di misticanza

MICRO GREEN SALAD WITH HAZELNUTS AND PECORINO

MISTICANZA is made up of micro greens and wild herbs, which, depending on the mixture, might be served raw or cooked. Market stalls sell it from beautiful tangled heaps of leafy greens, stems, and tendrils, which might feature arugula, dandelion greens, mustard leaves, borage, purslane, wild radish, chervil, fennel fronds, sorrel, cress, endive, nettles, or clover. Every field and farm provides its own unique *misticanza* mix, so feel free to create your blend depending on what's available to you. You can even visit your local farmers' market, or forage them yourself! Choose the youngest leaves of freshly picked wild greens. Be sure to use the best possible olive oil you can get your hands on and avoid too much acid, allowing the distinct flavors of the greens to stand out.

serves 4 to 6

1 pound freshly picked mixed wild greens

¼ cup hazelnuts, toasted and chopped

¼ cup extra-virgin olive oil

3 tablespoons fresh lemon juice (from 1 lemon)

Sea salt and freshly ground black pepper

Hard sheep's-milk cheese for shaving (we like semi-aged pecorino from Lazio or Tuscany)

Trim the greens, removing any yellowed or darkened leaves. Tear any oversized leaves into bite-size pieces.

Place the greens in a large bowl and toss by hand with the hazelnuts, olive oil, lemon juice, and salt and pepper to taste. Use a vegetable peeler to shave slices of pecorino over the salad and serve immediately.

For a vegetarian version, simply leave out the *guanciale*. There are several traditional schools of thought on how *vignarola* should be made, and a version without *guanciale* is actually one of them.

vignarola

ARTICHOKE, PEAS, FAVA, AND LETTUCE STEW

APRIL IS a spectacular month for Roman produce; the highlight is *vignarola* season, the short window in which the dish's core components—lettuce, fava beans, artichokes, peas, and spring onions—are all in harmony. Traditionally, *vignarola* is not a vibrant green dish. It's more of a grayish, soft green, which is a result of cooking the different vegetables in liquid, introducing them in stages to accommodate their cooking times. Our spring stew is a modern version, less rustic and more verdant. Here, we blanch the favas and remove them from their outer shells, a step the old-school version would skip, but one that lends a tenderness and sweetness to the dish. The high heat helps to ensure that the vegetables cook quickly and maintain their individual flavors and textures, as each element should be soft but still have some inner firmness. Seasoning lightly after every addition ensures that each individual vegetable gets the love it needs. *Vignarola* improves overnight and will keep in the refrigerator for about three days.

serves 4 to 6 as a starter or side dish

1½ cups shelled fava beans (from about 2 pounds in pods)

¼ cup extra-virgin olive oil, plus more as needed

3½ ounces *Guanciale* (page 82) or pancetta, diced

2 garlic cloves, smashed

4 tender young globe artichokes, cleaned (see page 167) and quartered

Sea salt and freshly ground black pepper

6 sprigs fresh mint (see page 142)

½ cup dry white wine

Water or Vegetable Broth (recipe follows)

1½ cups fresh or frozen shelled peas (from about 2 pounds in pods)

Fill a medium bowl with ice and water. Bring a medium pot of water to a boil over high heat. Blanch the fava beans in the boiling water for 1 minute, in batches, if necessary, to avoid overcrowding. Drain and immediately plunge them into the ice water bath. Remove and discard the bitter skins by squeezing each fava bean gently between your fingers. Small fava beans can be left whole. Set aside.

Heat the olive oil in a large skillet over low heat. When the oil begins to shimmer, add the *guanciale*. Cook until the fat turns translucent, then add the garlic. Cook until just fragrant, then immediately drain the artichokes and add them to the pan along with a generous pinch of salt, pepper, and half the mint, stirring to coat.

Increase the heat to high and add the wine. Simmer until the alcohol aroma dissipates, about a minute, then add enough water or broth to cover the artichokes halfway. Cook until the artichokes begin to soften, 10 to 12 minutes, then add the peas, fava beans, and spring onions. Season again with salt

RECIPE CONTINUES

4 spring onions or scallions (white parts only), thinly sliced

1 small head romaine lettuce, shredded crosswise into ½-inch strips (4 cups)

1½ tablespoons lemon juice (from ½ lemon; optional)

and pepper. Continue to cook until the peas are soft, about 10 minutes, stirring frequently, adding more vegetable broth or water as needed to keep the vegetables in a bit of simmering liquid.

Add the lettuce, stir to combine, and cook for 5 minutes more, or until all the components are fully cooked and tender. Remove the pot from the heat, season the stew with lemon juice, if desired, and garnish with the remaining mint. Serve warm or room temperature, or even the following day.

brodo vegetale

VEGETABLE BROTH

makes 1 quart

2 cups empty pea pods

4 artichoke stems

4 spring onions or scallions (green parts only)

Set aside the pea pods, artichoke stems, and the green stalks from the spring onions from the *Vignarola* (page 155). Place in a medium pot and add cold water to cover. Bring to a boil over medium heat, reduce the heat to maintain a simmer, and cook for 10 minutes, then drain. No need to season with salt or pepper.

pomodori con riso

BAKED TOMATOES STUFFED WITH RICE

STUFFED TOMATOES, often baked with diced potatoes, are a summer staple in Rome, turning up in every imaginable dining setting. They are as at home at a rustic picnic in the Caffarella Park as they are on a restaurant menu. They are a favorite of home cooks and restaurants, and also figure heavily into the city's "fast-food" options. They are always prepared in advance and served at room temperature.

makes 6 **pomodori con riso**

¼ cup extra-virgin olive oil

6 ripe but firm medium tomatoes

1 garlic clove, smashed

1 cup Arborio or Carnaroli rice

6 large fresh basil leaves

½ cup grated Pecorino Romano

1 large potato, peeled and cut into 1-inch pieces

Sea salt and freshly ground black pepper

Preheat the oven to 350°F.

Evenly drizzle 1 tablespoon of the olive oil over the bottom of a shallow, medium ovenproof casserole dish.

Remove and reserve the tops of the tomatoes. Using a small spoon or straight paring knife, over a bowl, carefully remove and reserve the soft insides of the tomatoes, taking care to leave the ribs separating the seed segments intact. Puree the juice and pulp with an immersion blender or in a food processor and set aside.

Bring a pot of water to a boil over high heat. Meanwhile, heat 2 tablespoons of the olive oil in a shallow, medium pan over low heat. When the oil begins to shimmer, add the garlic and cook until it just begins to turn golden, about 5 minutes, then add the tomato juice and the rice. Cook until the rice is very al dente (see page 34), about 20 minutes, adding boiling water, ¼ cup at a time, if it begins sticking to the pan. Remove the pan from the heat and stir in the basil and the Pecorino Romano. Season to taste.

Lightly salt the inside of each tomato, then fill three-quarters of the way with the rice mixture. Stand the tomatoes upright in the prepared casserole dish and fill in the space around them with the diced potatoes. Drizzle the remaining olive oil over the tomatoes and add a splash of water to the bottom of the dish.

Bake until the rice is cooked through, about 45 minutes. Begin checking on the tomatoes after 30 minutes, adding water as necessary to keep the bottom from burning. Remove from the oven and allow to cool, about 20 minutes. Serve at room temperature.

THE MERCATO

SOME OF Rome's 120 city-run markets, called *mercati rionali*, are housed in bizarrely modern structures that could pass for suburban American office buildings. Others are obscured behind brick and limestone facades designed in a rational, Fascist style. The most conspicuous fill the city's cobblestoned piazzas, concrete sidewalks, and asphalt streets; they're the ones you probably picture when you imagine a Roman market.

Aside from their obvious aesthetic differences, what sets each *mercato rionale* apart is the nature of its location. Rome's neighborhoods each have a distinct character mirrored in their market spaces. Piazza Vittorio's market, a social hub for immigrants, sells exotic produce and spices alongside local Roman items. Trionfale's, heavily frequented by a budget-conscious aging population, features butchers alongside stalls devoted to shoe repair or selling cheap underwear. In Testaccio (see page 132), nearly a dozen stalls offer takeaway meals—a rarity for a market—in order to attract students from the growing university next door.

The *mercati rionali* are as much commercial places as they are social, providing an aging clientele—half are over sixty years old— spaces to interact with others and with stall vendors to whom they have become loyal. And just as important, the spaces provide employment, though statistics show that market occupancy has dwindled considerably in recent decades.

Due to the mature shopping demographic—8 in 10 are forty-six years old or older—the city's markets must be dynamic if they hope to survive in the future. The inherently bureaucratic nature of city-run sites means the market vendors can't always respond to client demand in real time, and limited market hours lead employed Romans to choose supermarkets over *mercati rionali*. Is the Roman market in its death throes? We hope not, but it isn't beyond the realm of possibility.

For the city's market culture to survive, it must appeal to a younger demographic—and a new model has entered the equation in the past decade: the farmers' market. Most *mercati rionali* stalls are staffed by middlemen; the farmers' markets provide farm-direct sales and are open on weekends only. This latter fact alone makes them appealing, since

mercati rionali are generally open only in the morning, Monday through Saturday. At farmers' markets you are naturally more likely to find local food for sale, where much of the produce at the *mercati rionali* is imported from Campania, Puglia, Sicily, and Sardinia. To stress their local affiliations, farmers' markets advertise that their products come from no more than 100 kilometers (62 miles) from the point of sale, calling them "km 0," a buzzword that has become synonymous with locavore cuisine.

Whether the farmers' market and "km 0" phenomena will survive the test of time remains to be seen, in Rome and elsewhere. But as long as *mercati rionali* adapt to their surroundings and the needs of their customers, as those of Piazza Vittorio, Trionfale, and Testaccio have, they will remain an indelible symbol of Rome's celebrated market tradition.

verdure gratinate al forno

BAKED VEGETABLES WITH BREAD CRUMBS

THIS SIMPLE and versatile recipe, as common on Roman *antipasti* buffets as on the home table, can be served as a starter or a side dish. What really transforms it is cooking the vegetables beyond the point of al dente. Romans may insist that their pasta maintains a serious bite, but their vegetables almost always must be well-done. Resist the temptation to take the baking sheet out of the oven when the vegetables look cooked— allow them to roast a bit longer in a liberal dousing of olive oil until they are soft and caramelized.

serves 4 to 6 as a starter or side dish

2 red bell peppers, cut into ½-inch-thick strips

2 white onions, cut into ½-inch-thick rings

2 zucchini, cut lengthwise into ¼-inch-thick slices

1 eggplant, cut crosswise into ¼-inch-thick rounds

1 tablespoon sea salt

½ cup extra-virgin olive oil

2 cups Seasoned Bread Crumbs (recipe follows)

Preheat the oven to 350°F.

On a parchment paper–lined baking sheet or in an unlined casserole dish, toss the vegetables with the salt, then with ¼ cup of the olive oil. Layer the bread crumbs on top, at least ¼ inch thick.

Drizzle over the remaining ¼ cup olive oil and bake, covered with aluminum foil, for 30 to 40 minutes, until the vegetables have reduced in size considerably. Uncover and continue to bake until the vegetables are soft, 20 to 30 minutes more.

Serve hot.

pane grattugiato

SEASONED BREAD CRUMBS

makes 2 cups

8 to 10 slices dry country bread, torn into bite-size pieces

2 teaspoons dry oregano or chopped fresh flat-leaf parsley

2 tablespoons grated Pecorino Romano, Parmigiano-Reggiano, or Grana Padano

Preheat the oven to 250°F.

Spread the bread pieces on a rimmed baking sheet and bake until crispy and completely dried out, 15 to 20 minutes. Remove from the oven, allow to cool, and pulse in a food processor until finely ground to the size of coarse coffee grounds.

In a medium bowl, combine the bread crumbs with the oregano and grated cheese. Mix thoroughly.

The seasoned bread crumbs will keep in an airtight container for 1 or 2 days.

insalata di carciofi crudi

SHAVED ARTICHOKE SALAD

ROMANS TYPICALLY cook the tender inner leaves, hearts, and stems of artichokes, but wine bars, many of which lack a full kitchen, have taken to serving raw artichoke salads as a fresh, crisp, and flame-free alternative. The texture is best when the artichokes are sliced as thinly as possible, ideally on a mandoline. Their slightly sweet, bitter, and nutty flavors pair well with the tangy lemon juice and a hard cow's-milk cheese.

serves 4 to 6

3 tablespoons fresh lemon juice (from 1 lemon), plus more to taste

4 tender young artichokes, cleaned (see below)

¼ cup extra-virgin olive oil

Sea salt and freshly ground black pepper

1 tablespoon fresh mint leaves

Parmigiano-Reggiano or Grana Padano, for shaving

Put the lemon juice in a medium bowl and set aside.

Remove each artichoke individually from the lemon water and halve them. Using a teaspoon or melon baller, scoop out and discard the fuzzy inner choke and trim off any rough, pointy bits.

Slice each artichoke half into the thinnest possible wedges, then add them to the bowl with lemon juice and mix well. Slice the trimmed stems into the thinnest possible rounds and add to the bowl. Add the olive oil and salt and pepper to taste and mix well.

Garnish with the mint leaves. Use a vegetable peeler to shave slices of Parmigiano-Reggiano over the salad. Serve immediately.

Rome's local artichoke, called *carciofo romanesco*, is a staple that floods market stalls from December until May and appears on tables as a starter or a side dish. If you can't find them, substitute young, tender artichokes, ideally fresh and in season. You may need to adjust seasonings to accommodate. In Rome, they are available already cleaned and pruned, but you'll likely need to do this yourself.

Begin by filling a large bowl with cold water. Add the juice of 1 lemon and drop in the squeezed lemon halves. Snap off the tough outer leaves of each artichoke just above the base, one at a time. Continue to remove the layers until you reach the light-colored inner leaves. Cut off the stem, leaving about 1 inch attached to the base. Using a small knife with a short, thin blade, or a vegetable peeler, peel off the fibrous outer skin from the removed stem until you reach the pale green inner flesh. Drop it in the bowl with lemon water.

Carefully peel away the tough, dark green skin from the base of the artichoke and its trimmed stem. Remove and discard the upper cone of leaves. Hold in the lemon water to prevent oxidizing until ready to use.

---

verdura ripassata in padella

TWICE-COOKED GREENS

THIS RECIPE works with an array of leafy greens such as dandelion greens, chard, beet greens, mustard greens, curly endive, broccoli rabe, or escarole, any of which you can use individually or mix together. The greens may be wild or cultivated, but the basic method won't change. Romans often cook leafy vegetables in two stages: first, to tenderize the tougher stems, reduce bitterness, and make the leaves easier to work with, they parboil the greens; then to cook further and impart additional flavor, they sauté them in olive oil with garlic and *peperoncino*. *Verdura ripassata in padella* is served as a *contorno*, a vegetable side dish that accompanies the main course.

serves 4 to 6 as a side dish

Sea salt

2 pounds greens of your choice

½ cup extra-virgin olive oil

2 garlic cloves, smashed

½ teaspoon *peperoncino* or red pepper flakes

———————◆———————

To bring down the temperature of the greens faster, spread them out on a baking sheet. It will halve the cooling time.

———————◆———————

Bring a large pot of water to a boil over high heat. Salt the water. When the salt has dissolved, add the greens. Boil for 5 to 10 minutes, until the greens are cooked through and beyond the point of al dente; the amount of time will depend on the type of green and the thickness of the stalks. Drain and set aside to cool, about 20 minutes. When the greens are cool enough to handle, squeeze out any excess water.

Heat the olive oil in a large skillet over medium heat. When the oil begins to shimmer, add the garlic and cook just until it begins to just turn golden, about 5 minutes, then add the *peperoncino*. Cook until fragrant, about 30 seconds, then add the boiled greens and turn to coat. Season with salt. Cook, stirring frequently, for 8 to 10 minutes, until the greens have darkened and absorbed the garlic and *peperoncino* flavors.

Serve warm or at room temperature.

insalata di rughetta e pinoli

ARUGULA AND PINE NUT SALAD

THIS SIMPLE side salad was inspired by a stroll on the Palatine Hill, where, legend has it, Romulus founded the city of Rome on April 21, 753 BC. Of course there's no evidence to support this birthdate, nor the existence of Romulus, for that matter, but when the emperors rose to power, they built lavish villas around the reputed hut of the city's founding father. Today, the archeological park is dominated by nature. Visitors who trek up to the top of the Palatine Hill tread over peppery arugula, which grows wild among the ruins, and seek shade under towering pines that give way to olive and citrus groves.

serves 4 to 6

1 pound arugula

¼ cup pine nuts, toasted

3 tablespoons extra-virgin olive oil

1½ tablespoons fresh lemon juice (from ½ lemon)

Sea salt and freshly ground black pepper

In a large bowl, combine the arugula, pine nuts, olive oil, lemon juice, and salt and pepper to taste and toss with your hands. Serve immediately.

Pine nuts can be very expensive, so take care when you toast them, as there is a fine line between toasting and burning. Place them in a small cold pan over medium heat and stir continuously as they heat. When they get shiny, oily, and a little bit golden, 3 to 4 minutes, remove them from the pan and set aside to cool.

insalata di finocchio, radicchio, e pera

FENNEL, RADICCHIO, AND PEAR SALAD

THE CITY'S market stalls are certainly rich in local produce, but vendors don't deal exclusively in regional products. In the winter, the city is inundated with bitter radicchio varieties from the Veneto region of northern Italy, which pair well both flavor-wise, as well as aesthetically, with local fennel bulbs. This salad unites Rome's own fennel with northern Italian products, which are beloved by locals. The pear adds a pleasant sweetness to the mix.

serves 4 to 6

¼ cup plus 1 tablespoon extra-virgin olive oil

1 tablespoon fresh lemon juice

2 tablespoons balsamic vinegar

1 medium head radicchio, quartered, cored, and sliced crosswise into ½-inch strips

1 small fennel bulb, with fronds attached

1 small, firm pear (we like Comice or Bartlett), cored and cut into ⅛-inch slices

Sea salt and freshly ground black pepper

Leaves from 3 sprigs fresh flat-leaf parsley

1¾ ounces hard sheep's-milk cheese (we like semi-aged pecorino from Lazio or Tuscany)

In a large bowl, whisk together the olive oil, lemon juice, and vinegar to make the dressing and set aside.

Add the radicchio to the bowl with the dressing.

Slice the tops off the fennel, reserving any fronds. Halve the bulb, remove any tough outer layers, and soak in cold water just to release any dirt from between the layers. Pat dry, remove and discard the core, then slice thinly on a mandoline. Add to the bowl with the dressing and radicchio. Add the pear, tossing to coat, and season to taste.

Arrange the salad on a platter and garnish with the parsley leaves and reserved fennel fronds. Using a vegetable peeler, shave the cheese over the top and serve.

BREAD
AND PIZZA

Wherever you are in Rome, a bakery or pizzeria
isn't far away. The city has a carby culture, but
there aren't as many home bakers as you might
expect. Kitchens are small and bread baking and
pizza making are crafts that Romans entrust to
professionals. You certainly don't need to be an
expert to execute our baking recipes here, but you
will need a few simple tools, a digital scale, and a
love of the metric system. For the best results, we
practically insist you use the metric measurements
we list in the recipes. Do that and you're just a
long, slow ferment away from a slice of Rome.

pizza bianca e pizza rossa

SHEET PAN PIZZA TWO WAYS

PIZZA BIANCA (literally, white pizza) and *pizza rossa* (red pizza) are staples in the Roman diet. Both are simple snacks that can be wrapped in paper, carried away from a bakery, and eaten on the go. Either can substitute the *cornetto* breakfast pastry in the morning, or accompany a beer or cocktail in the evening. We love ordering a slice from Forno Campo de' Fiori in the late morning and taking it to nearby Piazza Farnese for a snack with a view over the cobblestoned square. These incredibly versatile flatbreads are made from the same dough, it's just their seasonings that differ: *pizza bianca* features extra-virgin olive oil and sea salt, while *pizza rossa* is brushed with a light tomato sauce and baked. The way they are consumed varies slightly as well. *Pizza bianca* can be sliced open to use as sandwich bread and filled with things like mortadella (referred to as *pizza cà mortazza* in local dialect—the quintessential Roman snack), prosciutto and mozzarella, and prosciutto with ripe figs. *Pizza rossa* is generally eaten on its own.

makes two 18 × 13-inch pizzas

FOR THE DOUGH

½ teaspoon (2 grams) active dry yeast

3½ cups (830 grams) cold water

7 cups plus 3 tablespoons (1,000 grams) high-quality bread flour

1 tablespoon plus 1 teaspoon (23 grams) sea salt

Neutral oil (see page 27), for greasing

1 cup (125 grams) durum flour or semolina, for dusting

Make the dough: In a small bowl, sprinkle the yeast over 2¾ cups (650 grams) water and set aside for a few minutes, until the yeast has dissolved.

Put the bread flour in a large bowl and add the yeast mixture. Stir with a spoon or with your hands until there is no more dry flour in the bowl and your dough is shaggy. Cover the bowl with plastic wrap and allow the dough to rise at room temperature for 30 minutes.

After 30 minutes, add the salt and remaining water and gently knead. Once all the water is incorporated, cover the bowl again with plastic wrap and allow the dough to rise for 30 minutes more.

Uncover the bowl. With one wet hand, lightly grasp one edge of the dough. Pull this flap of dough upward and outward, then attach it to the top of the dough. Turn the bowl a one-eighth turn and repeat until you have rotated the bowl a complete turn.

RECIPE CONTINUES

FOR PIZZA BIANCA

Extra-virgin olive oil, for drizzling

Sea salt

FOR PIZZA ROSSA

Salsa di Pomodoro **(recipe follows)**

Extra-virgin olive oil, for drizzling

Cover the bowl with plastic wrap again and repeat the folding procedure once every hour, three more times, allowing it to rest between each rotation.

After the last gentle folding, place the dough in a large, lightly greased bowl, cover it with plastic wrap, and set aside to rest for 30 minutes.

Meanwhile, cover a clean, dry work surface with a thick layer of durum flour. Grease two baking sheets and set aside. Preheat the oven to 480°F and set a baking stone, if using, in the oven to preheat as well.

When the dough is ready, carefully invert the bowl over the floured work surface, gently detaching the dough from the bowl with your fingers, if necessary. Dust the top of the dough well with durum flour, then very gently, taking care not to deflate the dough, put your hands underneath it, fingers pointing toward the center. Slowly pull the dough apart into a rectangle, then change direction and widen the strip with the same technique to create a 15-inch square.

Halve the dough and brush off any excess flour, then quickly and carefully transfer the two rectangles to the prepared baking sheets. Fit the dough to the baking sheets by gently pushing it with spread fingertips, moving from the center outward. If it springs back, allow it to rest for a few minutes before trying again. Set aside to rest on the baking sheets for 5 minutes.

To make *pizza bianca*, drizzle olive oil on top of the dough and season lightly with salt. Using your fingertips, make indentations all over the dough to distribute the air pockets evenly. To make *pizza rossa*, spread *salsa di pomodoro* over the dough in an even layer, leaving a small border uncovered around the edge. The dough will be lightly dressed.

Bake for 10 to 12 minutes, until the crust is golden with a few dark spots. Allow to cool on a wire rack for a few minutes.

Serve the *pizza bianca* in slices or slivers, or cut open and fill with mortadella or other cold cuts. For *pizza rossa*, drizzle extra-virgin olive oil on top of the tomato layer after baking. Serve in slices or slivers.

salsa di pomodoro

makes sauce for 2 lightly dressed pizze rosse

1 (14-ounce) can whole peeled tomatoes

1 tablespoon extra-virgin olive oil

2 teaspoons sea salt

In a medium bowl, combine the tomatoes, olive oil, and salt.

Using your hands or a fork, tear and squeeze the tomatoes to shred them. The sauce should be slightly chunky.

ROMAN BREADS, FLOURS, AND MILLS

SURVEYING the shelves of a bakery in Rome today, you will find loaves ranging from barely leavened, basic sandwich buns to naturally fermented whole-wheat loaves made with heirloom grains. Everyday bread is simple and unadorned, while at the holidays it's not unusual to find options incorporating walnuts, raisins, and even dried whole figs. For the most part, the quotidian standard is no-frills but satisfying enough, with a crusty exterior that gives way to soft and chewy insides.

The most common breads are *pane di Lariano*, a sourdough in the style of a nearby village of the same name, and *pane casareccio*, a rustic and unrefined loaf. Both are sliced and used as sponges to mop up the saucy or oily remains of a meal, a practice oddly known as *facendo la scarpetta*, which literally means "making a little shoe." *Tozzetti*, square buns with a thick and durable crust, do double duty as sauce catchers and sandwich holders, while *rosette*, *tartarughe*, and *Ciabattine* (page 192) are all exclusively sandwich breads with thin, pliable crusts.

To reproduce Roman-style bread at home, start with the types of grains and flours used in Rome. Molino Iaquone, a family-run mill near Viterbo, exports their products and sells them online. This mill specializes in tender wheat blends ideal for breads, pizzas, and rolls. Their flours are interchangeable with King Arthur Bread Flour, a versatile, high-protein product. When a recipe calls for heirloom wheat flour, Rome's top bakers turn to the Piedmont-based family venture Mulino Marino, and you can, too; Formaggio Kitchen and Eataly sell their flours online (see Resources, page 249). The Marinos work closely with small farms to source heirloom grains, which are stone-ground to various grades of fineness. South Carolina's Anson Mills also makes fabulous, high-quality flours, available via mail order, that can stand-in for Mulino Marino flours.

pizza romana

THIN CRUST ROMAN-STYLE PIZZA

UNLIKE the thick-rimmed Neapolitan style of pizza popular across the globe, Rome's version of the famous flatbread is thin and practically rimless. Most pizzerias prefer a quick, barely fermented dough. As a result, Roman-style pizza is relatively bland, as the yeast and flour don't have the time to work together to create complex flavors. Our version, not bogged down by a pizzeria's bottom line, uses a long, cold fermentation for results that are fragrant, crispy, and a bit chewy. The small amount of durum flour and the slow refrigerated rise give the crust its extra crunch and tastiness. Use a stand mixer to knead the dough, or budget 10 to 15 minutes for hand kneading. The final trick is to stretch or roll the pizza so the base is very thin. Then add the toppings of your choice. We suggest the Rome-inspired toppings that follow this recipe, but feel free to get creative.

makes four 12- to 15-inch pizzas

Pinch (½ gram) of active dry yeast

1 cup plus 3 tablespoons (280 grams) cold water

3¼ cups (450 grams) bread flour

¼ cup plus 2 tablespoons (50 grams) durum wheat flour, plus more for dusting

2 teaspoons (12 grams) sea salt

2 teaspoons (12 grams) extra-virgin olive oil, plus more for greasing

Neutral oil (see page 27), for brushing

In a small bowl, sprinkle the yeast over the water and set aside for a few minutes, until the yeast has dissolved.

In the bowl of a stand mixer fitted with the dough hook, combine the flours, then add the yeast mixture. Mix on the lowest speed until the dough comes together, about 3 minutes. Then rest the dough, still in the mixer, for 5 minutes. Add the salt and mix on medium speed for 4 minutes, or until the dough is smooth and has developed good elasticity. With the mixer running on medium speed, slowly add the oil and mix until incorporated.

Cover the bowl with plastic wrap and allow the dough to rest for 30 minutes at room temperature.

Turn the dough out onto a lightly floured surface and cut it into four even pieces with a dough scraper or knife.

Working with one piece of dough at a time, take four edges and pull and fold them into the center. Do not flatten. The dough will tighten up and take on a round shape. Flip the dough, seam-side down, on the work surface. Place the palm of your hand on top of the ball, resting your thumb and pinkie

RECIPE CONTINUES

A baking stone will give your pizza a better crust, better volume, and incomparable lightness. If you do not have one, an inverted baking sheet or unglazed quarry tiles will work as substitutes. For the best results, preheat the stone or inverted baking sheet on the second-to-top rack for at least 45 minutes before baking. Recipe cooking times depend upon your baking surface and will be shorter if you use a stone.

against the sides and your other fingertips on the counter. Gently move the ball in circles, taking care to prevent any tears. You will feel the dough tighten further. Repeat this process with the remaining dough pieces.

Place the shaped dough balls on a greased baking sheet. Brush lightly with neutral oil and cover the whole baking sheet with plastic wrap. Transfer to the refrigerator and allow the dough to cold-rise for 24 hours.

Three hours before baking, remove the dough from the refrigerator and allow it to come to room temperature, still covered. The dough will rise slightly as it warms.

Preheat the broiler to high and set an inverted baking sheet or baking stone on the second highest rack in the oven to preheat as well.

Place one dough ball on a well-floured surface, then sprinkle more flour on top. Work the dough into a small disk by pushing your fingertips near the center of the dough and radiating outward toward the edges, leaving the center just slightly higher. Continue until you have a round disk about 6 inches in diameter and ¼ inch thick. Flip over the disk and move it to a portion of the work surface that is just lightly floured. Place both hands on top, palms down, side by side. Use one hand to anchor the dough and working slowly and carefully, use the other to gently push and stretch the dough away from the center. Turn a quarter turn and repeat, repositioning your hands each time. Continue until the disk is 12 to 15 inches in diameter and as thin as possible without tearing. Alternatively, use a rolling pin to achieve desired dimensions.

Transfer the shaped dough to a pizza peel or a parchment paper–lined inverted baking sheet. Add your toppings (see pages 184–185) and transfer the pizza to the preheated baking sheet or baking stone. Bake until the crust is crisp and the toppings are cooked, 8 to 9 minutes. If baking without toppings, drizzle with olive oil before baking and remove the pizza from the oven as it begins to brown, 5 to 6 minutes, then season with salt to taste.

Repeat with the remaining dough balls. Serve immediately after baking.

patate e gricia

POTATO-GRICIA

toppings for 1 pizza

1 teaspoon extra-virgin olive oil

1½ ounces *Guanciale* (page 82), cut into ⅛-inch-thick tiles

1 potato, boiled, peeled, and crumbled

1 ounce grated Pecorino Romano

2½ ounces mozzarella, torn or cut into ½-inch pieces

Freshly ground black pepper

Heat the olive oil in a small pan over medium heat. When it begins to shimmer, add the *guanciale*. Cook, stirring frequently, until lightly browned. Transfer to paper towels to drain for a few minutes.

Distribute the *guanciale*, potato, Pecorino Romano, mozzarella, and pepper evenly over the shaped dough. Continue with the recipe.

prosciutto e fichi

PROSCIUTTO AND FIG

toppings for 1 pizza

3 very ripe figs

1½ ounces goat cheese

3 slices prosciutto

After baking the plain, olive-oil-drizzled dough, use your hands to smear the ripe figs over the surface of the pizza. Distribute bite-size pieces of goat cheese over the figs, and then lay the prosciutto over the toppings. Serve immediately.

fiori di zucca

SQUASH BLOSSOMS

toppings for 1 pizza

2½ ounces mozzarella, torn or cut into ½-inch pieces

4 squash blossoms, trimmed and opened

Distribute the mozzarella evenly over the shaped dough and lay the squash blossoms on top. Continue with the recipe.

capricciosa

MUSHROOM, ARTICHOKE, EGG, AND PROSCIUTTO

toppings for 1 pizza

½ cup tomato sauce

2½ ounces mozzarella, torn or cut into ½-inch pieces

2 button mushrooms, thinly sliced

3 olives

1 marinated artichoke heart, quartered

1 large egg

1 slice prosciutto

Spoon the tomato sauce over the pizza dough, leaving a ½-inch border, then distribute the mozzarella evenly. In quadrants, distribute the sliced mushrooms; the olives and artichoke; and leave the third and fourth empty. Continue with the recipe, then after 6 or 7 minutes of baking, remove the pizza from the oven, break an egg onto the third quadrant, and return to the oven to finish cooking, 1 minute more. When the pizza is cooked and the egg is still slightly runny, removed it from the oven, lay a slice of prosciutto over the fourth quadrant, and serve immediately.

pizzette

LITTLE PUFF PASTRY PIZZAS

THESE SIMPLE and savory puff pastry snacks pair perfectly with a fresh beer or craft cocktail (see page 227). They are sold by weight at bakeries, and you might also find a few complimentary *pizzette* if you order an apéritif at a bar or café, much like a bowl of peanuts at an American bar—but better.

makes 32 pizzette

⅓ cup tomato paste

3 tablespoons extra-virgin olive oil

½ teaspoon sea salt

½ teaspoon dried oregano (optional)

1 pound rough puff pastry, homemade (recipe follows) or store-bought

Preheat the oven to 400°F. Line a baking sheet with parchment paper.

In a small bowl, stir together the tomato paste, olive oil, salt, oregano (if using), and 2 to 3 tablespoons water to make a thick but brushable liquid.

Roll out the puff pastry into a rectangle that is approximately 10 × 20 inches and ¼ inch thick. Using a 2½-inch round cookie cutter, cut out thirty-two *pizzette*. Place on the prepared baking sheet, leaving about ¼ inch between each. Place any that don't fit on the tray in the refrigerator until you are ready to bake them. Brush the center of each *pizzetta* with the tomato paste, leaving a small border around the edge.

Bake for 12 to 15 minutes, or until the *pizzette* puff up and turned golden. Transfer to a serving tray and bake the remaining *pizzette*.

Serve immediately, or allow to cool to room temperature and store in an airtight container for up to 3 days.

rough puff pastry

makes 2 pounds 3 ounces (1 kilogram) puff pastry

4 cups (500 grams) all-purpose flour, plus more for dusting

1 teaspoon (5 grams) sea salt

Sift the flour and salt onto a clean, dry surface and make a well in the middle. Add the butter to the well and begin to work the butter into the flour by hand, squeezing the pieces flat as you go. Continue to mix quickly and lightly with your fingertips until the butter is grainy and resembles flour-covered cornflakes in spots.

2 cups plus 3 tablespoons (500 grams) cold unsalted butter, cut into ½-inch pieces

1 cup (240 grams) ice-cold water

Sprinkle half the ice water over the mixture and gather the dough into a ball. Add additional water by the teaspoon until a shaggy dough forms. (You may not need all the water.)

Wrap the dough in plastic wrap and chill in the refrigerator for 30 minutes.

Remove the dough from the refrigerator and, on a lightly floured surface, working in only one direction, roll the dough into a rectangle that is approximately 16 × 8 inches.

With one short edge facing you, fold the top third farthest from you toward the middle, and then the bottom third over that. Turn the dough clockwise a quarter turn, so that an open side faces you. Repeat the rolling-and-turning process. Wrap the dough in plastic wrap and chill in the refrigerator for 30 minutes.

Repeat the rolling and folding process one more time and allow the dough to chill for at least 30 minutes in the refrigerator before using. It will keep for up to 3 days in the refrigerator or up to 4 weeks in the freezer.

pizza al contrario

UPSIDE-DOWN PIZZA

GABRIELE BONCI is Rome's most famous pizza innovator. Once he mastered the art of pizza-making at Pizzarium near the Vatican, he began stretching the definition of the classic snack by putting his heirloom wheat–based, long-leavened, high-hydration dough to all sorts of new uses. From the man who brought you the pizza stuffed with a whole beef tongue comes the upside-down pizza; Bonci bakes his pizza toppings beneath the dough, so the crust is essentially aromatized and lightly steamed, infusing it with the flavor of the toppings. He inverts the pizza before serving. The name might sound gimmicky, but the concept is actually quite simple—and the flavor is amazing, so we adapted Bonci's upside-down pizza for home baking. It is especially delicious with oniony and other fragrant vegetal and herbal "toppings." The dough cold rises for 12 hours before baking, so take that into consideration before diving in. The time investment is worth the payoff!

makes one 18 × 13-inch pizza

FOR THE PIZZA

¾ teaspoon (3 grams) active dry yeast

1⅔ cups (400 grams) cold water

4 cups (500 grams) einkorn flour, plus more for dusting

2½ teaspoons (15 grams) sea salt

2 tablespoons (28 grams) extra-virgin olive oil, plus more for greasing

FOR THE TOPPINGS

5 springs fresh thyme

4 white onions, sliced

Sea salt and freshly ground black pepper

¼ cup extra-virgin olive oil

Make the pizza: In a small bowl, sprinkle the yeast over 1½ cups (350 milliliters) of the cold water. Set aside for a few minutes until the yeast dissolves.

Place the flour in a large bowl, then add the yeast mixture. Mix with your hands or a wooden spoon just until the flour is hydrated. Cover the bowl with plastic wrap and allow the dough to rest for 20 minutes at room temperature.

Add the salt, remaining water, and the oil to the rested dough and mix by hand or with a wooden spoon just until combined. Shape the dough roughly into a ball and place it in a greased plastic container or bowl. Cover tightly with plastic wrap and set aside to rise in the refrigerator at about 40°F for 6 hours.

Remove the dough from the refrigerator and uncover the bowl. With one wet hand, lightly grasp one edge of the dough. Pull this flap of dough upward and outward, then attach it to the top of the dough. Turn the bowl a one-eighth turn and repeat until you have rotated the bowl a complete turn. Cover the bowl with plastic wrap again and return to the refrigerator to chill for 6 hours more.

Remove the dough and allow it to come to room temperature, about 30 minutes.

Preheat the oven to 480°F and position a rack in the middle.

Line a baking sheet with parchment paper and distribute the thyme, onions, and salt and pepper to taste evenly over the parchment paper. Drizzle with the olive oil and toss with your hands, distributing the "toppings" evenly across the parchment.

Invert the bowl with the dough over a clean, dry, floured surface and gently help the dough detach from the bowl with your hands. Dust the top of the dough with more flour. Using your fingertips, carefully push and stretch the dough into the shape of the baking sheet, taking care not to tear it. Transfer the dough on top of the ingredients, gently stretching it a bit more if necessary to cover them. Repair any holes. Cover the baking sheet with plastic wrap and allow it to rise at room temperature for 20 minutes.

Transfer to the oven and bake on the middle rack until the dough turns golden, about 20 minutes. Remove the pizza from the oven and allow it to cool slightly, about 5 minutes. Invert the baking sheet onto a large cutting board or platter. Remove the parchment. Slice and serve.

i cracker

CRACKERS

IN THE SOUTH of Italy, drinks are served with dry, round crackers called *taralli*. These savory rings, much like salted peanuts, make you thirsty for more. Aside from being a stellar mechanism to drive alcohol sales, this crunchy snack is a pleasant accompaniment to a cold beer. Our crackers riff on the flavors of *taralli*, but transform the round form into a thin and crispy cracker. Use a pasta machine to achieve maximum thinness, or you can use a rolling pin.

makes 8 crackers

1¼ teaspoons (5 grams) active dry yeast

¼ cup plus 1 tablespoon (90 milliliters) warm water (105°F to 115°F)

2 cups plus 3 tablespoons (300 grams) all-purpose flour, plus more for dusting

1 teaspoon (5 grams) sea salt

Flavorings of your choice (optional; see variations below)

2 tablespoons (28 grams) extra-virgin olive oil

TO MAKE BLACK PEPPER CRACKERS, add 1 tablespoon coarsely ground black pepper to the sifted flour and salt.

TO MAKE *PEPERONCINO* CRACKERS, add 1 tablespoon *peperoncino* or red pepper flakes to the sifted flour and salt.

TO MAKE ROSEMARY CRACKERS, add 1 tablespoon finely chopped fresh rosemary to the sifted flour and salt.

In a small bowl, sprinkle the yeast over the warm water and set aside until it has dissolved, about 10 minutes.

In a medium bowl or on the countertop, sift together the flour and salt, then mix with flavorings, if desired. Make a well in the center. Pour the olive oil into the well along with an additional 5 tablespoons water, then add the yeast mixture. Mix with your hands to pull together a ball of dough.

Transfer to a lightly floured surface and knead for a few minutes, until the dough is supple and smooth. Form into a ball, cover it with an inverted medium bowl, and allow to rest for 30 minutes.

Preheat the oven to 400°F. Line a baking sheet with parchment paper.

Cut the dough into eight equal pieces. Flatten one piece with your hands and lightly dust with flour, leaving the remaining dough under the bowl until you're ready to use it. Feed the dough through a pasta machine, starting on the largest setting, gradually reaching the thickness of four stacked playing cards. If you are using any flavorings in your dough, stop a setting or two before to prevent tearing. Place on the prepared baking sheet and repeat with the remaining dough.

Prick the dough with a fork or skewer to make small holes. Bake for 10 to 12 minutes, until the cracker has bubbled up and browned in places and is cooked through. Use immediately, or store in an airtight container at room temperature for up to 1 week.

ciabattina di passi

PASSI'S *CIABATTINA*

ENJOYING CLASSIC Roman main dishes like tripe, tongue, and oxtail in portable form is very new to Rome where, until recently, such specialties were served exclusively in homes or restaurants. Now a growing number of street food stalls and market vendors are serving hearty, homemade classics to go, using bread with a crisp exterior and absorbent interior to deliver their flavorful dishes. The finest incarnation of this new phenomenon is at Mordi e Vai in the Testaccio Market. There, Sergio and Mara Esposito use *ciabattine* from Panificio Passi in nearby Piazza Santa Maria Liberatrice. Our version has a little more complexity; the durum flour lends a nuttiness, while the extra-virgin olive oil gives softness and a better keeping quality. The honey imparts a subtle perfume and helps to balance the flavor of savory fillings like *Picchiapò* (page 84) and *Pollo alla Romana* (page 89), or acidic fillings such as *Concia* (page 109). Baking it at home saves you from the sharp elbows of the eager customers at Passi's bread counter, though, frankly, being jostled by octogenarian shoppers does have its charm.

makes 8 ciabattine

1 recipe *Biga* (page 196)

1 cup (240 grams) cold water

1¾ cups (250 grams) bread flour

¼ cup plus 2 tablespoons (50 grams) durum wheat flour, plus more for dusting

1 tablespoon (15 grams) extra-virgin olive oil, plus more for greasing

2½ teaspoons (15 grams) sea salt

1½ teaspoons (10 grams) honey

In a medium bowl, combine the *biga* and the water, mixing with your hands. The *biga* will not dissolve completely, but it will loosen and the water will become white and milky.

Add the bread flour, durum wheat flour, olive oil, salt, and honey to the bowl with the *biga*. Stir with your hands until there is no more dry flour in the bowl and the dough is shaggy. Cover the bowl with plastic wrap and allow the dough to rest at room temperature for 30 minutes.

Uncover the bowl. With one wet hand, lightly grasp one edge of the dough. Pull this flap of dough upward and outward, then attach it to the top of the dough. Turn the bowl a one-eighth turn and repeat until you have rotated the bowl a complete turn. Cover the bowl with plastic wrap again. Repeat the folding procedure once every 30 minutes, two more times.

Lightly oil a medium bowl. Add the dough, placing it smooth-side up. Cover with plastic wrap and set aside to rise at room temperature for 30 minutes.

Preheat the oven to 480°F and set a baking stone or inverted baking sheet (see page 182) in the oven to preheat as well.

Transfer the dough to a well-floured work surface by inverting the bowl and gently detaching it using your hands, if necessary. Flour the top of the dough well, then very gently, taking care not to deflate it, put your hands underneath, fingers pointing toward the center. Slowly move your hands apart, gently pulling the dough into a strip that is 4 inches wide and 15 inches long. Make a quarter turn and stretch it into a rectangle 8 inches wide, 15 inches long, and less than 1 inch thick. Allow the dough to rest for 5 minutes, then cut it in half lengthwise. Then cut each half crosswise into four equal-size rectangles using a dough scraper or a knife.

Carefully flip over one rectangle, then lift it and pull on the ends until it is about 6 inches long. Repeat with the remaining dough. Place each piece on a sheet of parchment paper, spacing them apart. Cover with plastic wrap and allow to rise for 20 minutes more.

Transfer the parchment paper with the dough onto the heated baking stone or inverted baking sheet. Using a spray bottle filled with water, spritz the dough about ten times, then close the oven door. Reduce the oven temperature to 400°F. After 3 minutes, spray the dough again. Bake for 18 to 20 minutes more, or until the bread is dark golden and feels light when lifted.

Remove the *ciabattine* from the oven and allow to cool on a wire rack until they reach room temperature, about 25 minutes. Use the same day, or freeze for up to 1 month. Thaw at room temperature for about 1 hour, then reheat in a preheated 300°F oven for 8 minutes.

trecce con olive, noci, e zucchine

OLIVE, WALNUT, AND ZUCCHINI TWISTY BREAD

TRECCE are twisted pieces of dough that come with assorted fillings. This recipe uses a baking technique known in Italy as *biga* (a type of "pre-ferment," in baking terms), which gives a more complex flavor and a more elastic dough. Plan ahead for this recipe, as the *biga* must be made the day before you plan to bake the *trecce*. We add a bit of dry yeast too, to help the fermenting get going.

makes 6 trecce, 2 of each flavor

FOR THE DOUGH

1 recipe *Biga* (recipe follows)

1⅔ cups (400 grams) warm water

¼ cup (50 grams) extra-virgin olive oil, plus more for greasing

¾ teaspoon (5 grams) malt syrup, or 2½ teaspoons (10 grams) sugar

4⅔ cups (650 grams) bread flour

1 teaspoon (4 grams) active dry yeast

2½ teaspoons (17 grams) sea salt

FOR THE FILLING

Extra-virgin olive oil

¼ teaspoon fresh rosemary, chopped

Pinch of *peperoncino* or red pepper flakes

2 small, firm zucchini, sliced crosswise as thinly as possible

Sea salt

½ cup olives, pitted and sliced

½ cup walnuts, lightly toasted and coarsely chopped

Make the dough: Combine the *biga*, water, olive oil, and malt syrup in a large bowl and mix with your hands for 5 minutes, breaking it up into pebble-size pieces. The mixture will be wet and lumpy. Combine the flour and yeast in a medium bowl, then add to the bowl with the *biga* mixture, stirring continuously with a wooden spoon until a sticky dough forms. Transfer to a clean, dry surface. Add the salt and work the dough with your hands for 5 minutes until it's tacky and soft. Return the dough to the bowl, cover with plastic wrap, and allow it to rise in a warm place for 1 hour, or until it has doubled in size.

Meanwhile, make the filling: Heat 1 tablespoon of olive oil in a small nonstick pan over medium-high heat. When the oil begins to shimmer, add the rosemary. When it sizzles, add the *peperoncino* and cook until fragrant, about 30 seconds, then add the zucchini and a pinch of salt. Cook until soft, 4 to 5 minutes. Remove the pan from the heat and set aside to cool.

Preheat the oven to 500°F. Oil two baking sheets.

Divide the dough into six equal pieces using a dough scraper or a knife. On a lightly floured surface, roll and stretch the dough into 24-inch long pieces, then dip your fingers in olive oil and gently press and stretch each piece into a long strip measuring about 2½ × 24 inches. Allow the dough to rest for 10 minutes.

Spread the sliced olives along the bottom half of the first two dough rectangles. Do the same with the chopped nuts on the next two, and the cooled zucchini filling on the last two.

RECIPE CONTINUES

You can fill the *trecce* directly on the baking sheets to avoid transferring and possibly losing filling.

To form each *treccia*, fold the dough over itself and its fillings. Pinch the open end to close, leaving the long sides open. Using both hands, twist the dough like you're gently wringing out a towel. Tuck in any filling that falls out; some of the filling should be visible.

Lightly brush the *trecce* with olive oil and allow to rest for 10 minutes.

Transfer the *trecce* to the prepared baking sheets, reduce the oven temperature to 450°F, and bake for 18 to 20 minutes, until lightly browned. Remove from the oven, brush lightly with oil, and season to taste. Serve immediately or store in a sealed container at room temperature for up to 3 days.

biga

1 teaspoon (3 grams) active dry yeast

½ cup (120 grams) filtered water

1¼ cups plus 3 tablespoons (200 grams) bread flour

In a small bowl, sprinkle the yeast over the water and set aside for a few minutes, until the yeast has dissolved.

In a medium bowl, combine the yeast mixture and flour, stirring well to incorporate, then knead by hand until the mixture becomes a homogeneous ball.

Place in a clean, lightly oiled medium bowl and cover with plastic wrap. Allow it to sit in the bottom (vegetable section) of the refrigerator for 12 hours. The *biga* should almost triple in size. If it does not, remove the bowl and allow to sit at room temperature until it has.

ROME'S PREEMINENT BAKERS

BESIDE ONE of Rome's busiest traffic circles sits the tomb of Marcus Vergilius Eurysaces, a freed slave and bread baker. As trams and commuter trains buzz past the two-thousand-year-old limestone building, bakers all over town knead and ferment dough as Eurysaces must have done so many centuries ago. Though little is known about him, we do know plenty about his industry. He likely relied on the mills built along the Tiber River and others powered by springs and aqueduct channels. His customers may have been on the dole; hundreds of thousands of Romans received free or subsidized grain, which bakers transformed into bread. He was probably baking from barley, rye, and emmer grown in southern Italy and North Africa. To permit such a tomb, his output must have been enormous and, based on the reliefs, which depict milling, kneading, stretching, and baking, Eurysaces ran a mill-to-table business. Feeding the ancient city's massive population—by the second century it had reached around I million residents—required a lot of bakers, and while few reached celebrity status, some evidently achieved notoriety and wealth.

Today, the relative number of bakeries has shrunk. Contemporary Romans have a richer diet than the ancients and therefore rely less on bread for sustenance. Small bakeries now compete with supermarkets, causing a crisis in the industry; rising real estate values have forced many bakeries to shutter in recent decades. In spite of these challenges, historic bakeries such as central Rome's Antico Forno Roscioli and Forno Campo de' Fiori have survived by diversifying their business, offering wholesale distribution as well as retail sales of bread, pizza by the slice, and prepared foods. In the case of both establishments, multigenerational family ownership has been critical to survival.

In the past few years, as celebrity chefs and TV food personalities have brought new attention to handmade foods, especially bread and pizza, Rome's new crop of bakers, like Gabriele Bonci and Stefano Preli, have capitalized on the dignity restored to the craft, opening eponymous shops that serve creations of their own design, which have earned them fame to rival even that of Eurysaces.

habemus panem di john regefalk

JOHN REGEFALK'S BREAD WITH FENNEL POLLEN
AND POPPY SEEDS

THIS NATURALLY leavened bread, created by chef and baker John Regefalk, is inspired by the flavors, form, and ingredients of Roman antiquity, hence the Latin name, a play on the *Habemus Papem*, the famous declaration when a new pope is elected. It draws on ancient grain varieties, similar to those Romans imported to the city from the fields of its vast empire, destined for rations and local bakeries. The segmented shape of the loaf is a throwback to the ancient custom of slicing loaves before baking to make them easier to tear into pieces in the absence of a bread knife. Note that the porridge must be prepared at least 12 hours ahead while a homemade liquid levain takes at least 1 week to develop. We've included a basic recipe for the latter, but you can also obtain liquid levain from most bakeries.

makes 2 loaves

FOR THE PORRIDGE

¾ cup plus 3 tablespoons (225 grams) boiling filtered water

1 cup plus 3 tablespoons (150 grams) whole-grain spelt flour

FOR THE BREAD

2¼ cups plus 3 tablespoons (300 grams) white spelt or emmer flour

3½ cups (500 grams) bread flour

¾ cup (200 grams) Liquid Levain (recipe follows)

2⅓ cups (570 grams) filtered water

1 teaspoon (5 grams) fennel pollen

1 tablespoon plus 1 teaspoon (23 grams) sea salt

¼ cup (30 grams) poppy seeds

Make the porridge: In a medium heatproof bowl, pour the boiling water over the flour. Stir with a wooden spoon until it binds together as a porridge. Allow to cool for 10 minutes, then cover with plastic wrap and set aside to rest at room temperature for 12 hours.

Make the bread: Once 12 hours have passed, mix the white spelt flour, bread flour, and liquid levain with 2 cups (470 grams) of the water in a large bowl. Cover the bowl with plastic wrap and allow to rest for 30 minutes.

Add the porridge, fennel pollen, salt, and remaining water to the dough and begin incorporating them slowly with your hands. Once the dough is smooth and well combined, cover the bowl with plastic wrap and allow the dough to rise at room temperature for about 30 minutes.

Uncover the bowl. With one wet hand, lightly grasp one edge of the dough. Pull this flap of dough upward and outward, then attach it to the top of the dough. Turn the bowl a one-eighth turn and repeat until you have rotated the bowl a complete turn.

Cover the bowl with plastic wrap again. Repeat the process two more times, resting the dough for 1 hour in between. After the third set of folds, allow the dough to rise for 1 hour more. Be

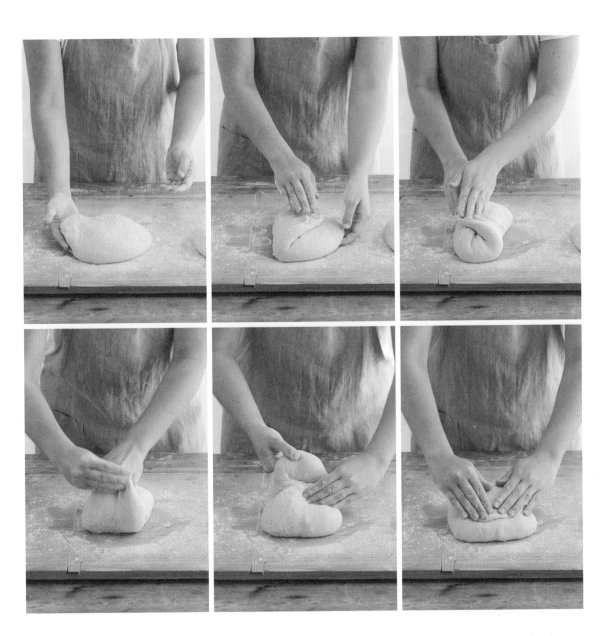

For the first two sets of folds on this dough, use normal force to help build a strong gluten network. As the dough traps air through fermentation, it will become puffier and the folds should become more gentle. Take care not to deflate it and undo what the yeast has accomplished.

gentle with the third set of folds, taking care not to deflate the dough. Allow the dough to rest for 1 hour more.

Invert the dough onto a well-floured work surface and gently detach it from the bowl using your hands. Halve the dough using a dough scraper or knife.

"Close" each piece of dough by folding its four sides, one by one, attaching the flaps to the top of the dough. Cover the two dough pieces directly on the work surface with plastic wrap and allow to rest for 15 minutes.

RECIPE CONTINUES

To give the loaves their final shape, place each piece of dough on a lightly floured surface, seam-side up. Brush off any excess flour. Work the dough in the same method as before, but "close" with eight folds instead of four. When the shaping is done, the loaf will have a round, slightly bulging form. Transfer the loaves, seam-side down, directly onto a parchment paper–lined pizza peel or inverted baking sheet. The loaves should be able to hold their bulging shape; if not, turn over again and give a few more folds to strengthen.

Using a spray bottle filled with water, lightly spritz the loaves and sprinkle poppy seeds on top. Cover with plastic wrap. Allow to rise at room temperature for 1 hour.

Preheat the oven to 480°F and set a baking stone or inverted baking sheet (see page 182) in the oven to preheat as well.

When the loaves have risen, uncover them and, using a dough scraper or knife, score them into six wedges each by pressing the dough scraper from the top down, taking care not to cut all the way through the loaf. Transfer the parchment paper with the loaves onto the preheated baking stone or baking sheet. Spritz each loaf about ten times each, then close the oven door. Reduce the oven temperature to 400°F. After 3 minutes in the oven, spritz the loaves another ten times each. Continue baking until the bread takes on a dark golden color, feels light when lifted, and makes a hollow sound when tapped on the bottom, about 1 hour.

Remove from the oven and allow to cool completely on a wire rack before slicing. This bread keeps well and will reach its height of fragrance only after cooling down completely, or even the next day.

liquid levain

3½ cups (500 grams) bread flour

3½ cups (500 grams) whole rye flour

In a large resealable container, combine the flours.

In a small glass bowl combine 200 grams room-temperature filtered water and 200 grams of the flour mixture and mix until smooth. Cover with a kitchen towel and allow the mixture to sit at warm room temperature for 48 hours.

After 48 hours have passed, check for signs of fermentation, such as bubbles, on the surface and around the edges of the mixture. Cover and allow to sit for another 24 hours. Check again to confirm that the bubbling has intensified. You should be able to smell the musty, acidic aromas of fermentation.

Place 25 grams of the fermented starter in a small bowl, discarding the rest. Add 50 grams of room-temperature filtered water and 50 grams of the reserved flour mixture and mix well. Cover and allow it to sit at warm room temperature for 24 hours.

Repeat the feeding and discarding process every 24 hours for about 1 week. You will observe a rise and fall cycle: volume will increase after feeding, then decrease. The aromas will change as well: at first funky and acidic, followed by pleasantly sour aromas reminiscent of yogurt. On the day prior to using, feed the starter twice, 12 hours apart.

The night before baking, prepare the levain: Put 1 teaspoon of the mature starter in a bowl. Add 100 grams room-temperature filtered water and 100 grams of flour blend. Mix well. Cover and allow to sit at room temperature until the next morning. Your levain is now ready for use.

Continue to perpetuate the remaining starter following the same base recipe of 25 grams mature starter blended with 50 grams each of filtered water and flour blend every 24 hours.

SWEETS

Rome's sweets aren't the most famous or elaborate in Italy—those would be Sicily's—but they are, nevertheless, available all over the city. *Sorbetto* and gelato are their own category, and they're best at the city's growing number of artisanal gelato shops (see page 211). Cookies, on the other hand, are sold at bakeries, while *Maritozzi con la Panna* (page 216) are reserved for pastry shops and old-school cafés. And of course, even something as simple as fruit can be enough to finish a meal, proved by the summertime classic peaches with wine, which we have transformed into a sorbet (see page 208).

CHIUSO

affogato al caffè

ZABAIONE GELATO DRENCHED IN COFFEE

THIS DESSERT is a simple one for which you can make everything from scratch, or "cheat" a bit and buy ice cream or gelato. A little something sweet, spiked with a shot of caffeine, is a nice way to end any meal. It's so easy: just scoop the boozy egg-based zabaione gelato into a cup, pour an espresso over it, and you've got an instant crowd-pleaser. Well, almost instant. You'll have to chill the zabaione mixture in the freezer for 6 hours before churning.

makes 6 to 8 **affogati**

5 large egg yolks

½ cup sugar

1½ cups whole milk

⅛ teaspoon sea salt

1½ cups heavy cream

¼ cup plus 3 tablespoons Marsala wine

1 freshly brewed espresso shot per person (¾ to 1 ounce)

If you don't have an ice cream maker, pour the chilled mixture into a gallon-size freezer bag and lay it flat on a tray. Freeze until solid, then break up the mixture into large chunks and blend in a food processor until smooth, working in batches if necessary. Transfer the mixture to a container with a lid and freeze until firm.

In a medium bowl, stir together the egg yolks and sugar. Using a handheld mixer or whisk, beat until pale yellow and thick, about 3 minutes.

In a medium saucepan, heat the milk and salt over low heat until very hot and steaming, but not boiling. Stir to prevent scalding. While beating at medium speed, add a small amount of the hot milk to the egg yolk mixture to temper it. Gradually pour the rest of the hot milk into the yolk mixture while still beating, then transfer the combined liquid back to the saucepan. Cook over low heat, stirring continuously with a heatproof spatula or wooden spoon, until the mixture begins to thicken and form a custard at 170°F, about 3 minutes. Test the custard by running your finger over the spatula or wooden spoon—it should leave a clean, solid line.

Remove the saucepan from the heat and strain the custard through a fine-mesh strainer into a medium bowl. Add the heavy cream and Marsala and stir well to combine. Allow the mixture to cool for a few minutes, then chill in the refrigerator for 6 hours or overnight. Freeze the mixture in an ice cream maker according to the manufacturer's instructions, or if you don't have one, see the tip at left.

To assemble the *affogato*: Scoop two small scoops of gelato into a short transparent glass. Make a shot of espresso and immediately pour it over the gelato. Serve immediately.

ROME'S CARNIVAL FOODS

STATE-SPONSORED partying has been a feature of Roman culture since the Republic, when pagan festivals encouraged the masses to misbehave, overeat, and drink during holidays like the Saturnalia. The upper class footed the bill, and such occasions maintained the delicate balance between the elite and the disenfranchised peasants.

During the papal era, too, festivals were a kind of reward to the peasant classes for their servitude. The religion may have changed since pagan times, but the need for cutting loose never waned. Among the state-sanctioned and state-funded parties was the Roman Carnival. At its thirteenth-century inception, it was a two-day affair of races and bull fights in Testaccio and Piazza Navona. But when the Venetian pope Paul II took the tiara in 1464, the festivities were stretched to nine days. Via del Corso, the mile-long road, hosted races of horses, donkeys, and water buffalo. Floats full of masked performers rode through the streets, and lavish banquets accompanied theatrical performances.

Today, few relics of this ritual remain. Rome's Carnival was banned in 1882 in order to suppress the city's religious orders. Recently, the (secular) city government tried to revive it, but the efforts failed miserably. But Romans do still celebrate Carnival in a way. Small children dress in costumes and toss fistfuls of paper confetti in the city's streets. Grown-up Rome dwellers queue at bakeries and pastry shops for sweets made only during Carnival. The most decadent treats are fried: chestnut-shaped *Castagnole* (page 207), dough balls, are rolled in sugar, while *frappe*, fried strips of dough, are dusted in confectioners' sugar or drizzled with honey. The form of these fritters has remained more or less the same for centuries. The only significant change has been in the fat used for frying. In the days when Romans would slaughter hogs in the winter, the city's Carnival treats were fried in lard. Bakeries today use vegetable oils, and a few offer baked versions for diet-conscious revelers.

Check the oil temperature every few minutes to make sure it doesn't get too hot, lest the outside of the *castagnole* brown too quickly, leaving the center uncooked. Take care not to overcrowd the pan.

castagnole

FRIED DOUGH BALLS WITH SUGAR

SO-CALLED because their size and shape evoke that of a chestnut (*castagna* in Italian), these fried balls of dough are sold at bakeries only in the days leading up to Lent.

makes 30 castagnole

3 cups all-purpose flour

3 large eggs

2 teaspoons baking powder

Pinch of baking soda

2 tablespoons fresh orange juice (from ½ orange)

½ teaspoon fresh lemon juice

3 tablespoons Sambuca

5 tablespoons sugar, plus more for coating

½ cup vegetable oil

½ cup whole milk

Neutral oil (see page 27), for frying

Mix the flour, eggs, baking powder, baking soda, orange juice, lemon juice, Sambuca, sugar, vegetable oil, and milk in a large bowl until smooth.

In a small pot or cast-iron skillet, heat 2½ inches of neutral oil to 350°F over medium heat. Using a teaspoon or small ice cream scoop, scoop up a spoonful of batter, then carefully scrape it off with a second teaspoon into the hot oil.

Cook the *castagnole* in batches of four or five for about 4 minutes, until a deep golden brown. Halfway through cooking, they will turn themselves over in the oil. Take care not to overcrowd the pan.

Remove to a paper towel–lined tray or plate to drain, then roll them in sugar while they are still hot so that the sugar sticks.

Castagnole are best eaten the day they are prepared, but they will keep in an airtight container at room temperature for 3 to 4 days.

sorbetto di pesche e vino

PEACH AND WINE SORBET

EVERY ROMAN gelato shop offers classics like *pistacchio*, *cioccolato*, *nocciola*, and *fragola*, but only one boozy flavor—zabaione, an egg yolk and Marsala wine custard—makes the list of standards. Recently, though, at a small but growing number of artisanal *gelaterie*, the selection has received a spirited makeover. At places like Il Gelato di Claudio Torcè, Fatamorgana, Otaleg, and Carapina, alcohol-based flavors are becoming increasingly common. These refreshing and boozy sweets are fairly easy to reproduce at home. This recipe, which is technically a sorbet due to the absence of dairy, is inspired by a common summer dessert, *pesche al vino*, in which a peeled peach marinates in wine. The sorbet mixture must rest for at least 6 hours in the refrigerator before churning.

makes 1 pint

2 cups diced peaches, plus 1 whole peach

3 tablespoons fresh lemon juice (from 1 lemon)

½ cup plus 1 tablespoon sugar

¼ cup plus 2 tablespoons dry white wine (we like Marco Carpineti's Capolemole)

2 sprigs fresh mint (optional)

In a medium bowl, combine the diced peaches and lemon juice and set aside.

Combine ½ cup of the sugar and ½ cup water in a small saucepan over low heat and stir until the sugar has dissolved. Remove from the heat and allow the syrup to cool to room temperature, about 20 minutes. Transfer the syrup to a food processor, add the diced peaches and lemon juice, and process until smooth. Add ¼ cup of the wine and process again, then chill the mixture in the refrigerator for at least 6 hours or overnight.

Freeze the mixture in an ice cream maker according to the manufacturer's instructions, or if you don't have one, see the tip on page 204. Meanwhile, peel and dice the whole peach and combine it in a small bowl with the remaining 1 tablespoon sugar and 2 tablespoons wine. Allow to macerate for at least 30 minutes.

Serve the sorbet garnished with the wine-macerated peach and mint (if using).

To cool the syrup more quickly, prepare an ice bath while the pan is over the heat. Once all the sugar has dissolved, remove the pan from the heat and place it in the ice bath.

NATURAL, ARTISANAL GELATO

IT'S EASY to get used to eating gelato every day—and it's one of the perks of living in Rome during its notoriously hot summers. Everyone else is doing it, so why not? But Romans, unlike other Italians, tend to eat a lot of gelato all year round. With around 2,500 *gelaterie* in town, there are many styles and flavors to choose from. But for anyone after truly exceptional quality, the selection may be a bit more limited.

For most gelato makers, quality isn't a priority. Instead, the bottom line wins out in a city of high rents and seemingly unlimited demand. During the past decade, the price of gelato has remained stable while the cost of its ingredients, not to mention the energy for refrigeration, has risen. Even the most famous and historic places have resorted to using industrial mixes and other substances engineered to create an affordable product. While gelato of the past always contained milk or cream, dehydrated milk powders and vegetable oils have entered the equation.

If all this sounds alarming, it should, but the unfortunate decline of Rome's gelato industry has a silver lining. A small but growing group is making all-natural gelato from excellent products like fresh, organic dairy, locally cultivated fruits, and exquisite chocolate. These *gelatai* aren't part of some elitist movement; they are humble, hardworking people who believe that providing a product made with natural ingredients is an obligation, not a choice.

The natural gelato makers of Rome offer all the classic flavors like *crema*, *cioccolato*, *stracciatella*, *pistacchio*, and seasonal fruit sorbets, but they also go beyond the obvious to infuse the *gelati* and *sorbetti* with their personal preferences. Claudio Torcè of Il Gelato di Claudio Torcè is a beer drinker, revealed by his cashew and double malt flavor. Herbs inspire Maria Agnese Spagnuolo of Fatamorgana, as evidenced by her almond milk, mint, and ginseng sorbet and basil and walnut gelato. Otaleg's Marco Radicioni shows his love of spirits in his boozy flavors, while Florentine Simone Bonini of Carapina uses sweet Tuscan wine in his rich, creamy *vin santo* flavor. With choices like these, how could anyone refuse a couple of scoops a day?

panna cotta alla menta con salsa di cioccolato

MINT PANNA COTTA

EVERY ROMAN restaurant serves panna cotta. The wobbly dairy dessert, typically doused in chocolate sauce or fruit syrup, is easy to reproduce at home. Here, we use mint, the ubiquitous local herb, for flavor, and top it with dark chocolate sauce for a bittersweet touch. You'll need 5½-ounce ramekins (see page 26) for this recipe—and plan in advance; the panna cotta should set in the refrigerator for at least 4 hours.

makes 4 panne cotte

FOR THE PANNA COTTA

1½ teaspoons unflavored granulated gelatin

1 (1-inch) vanilla bean

Handful of fresh mint leaves, plus more for garnish

3 tablespoons sugar

1 cup whole milk

1 cup heavy cream

Neutral oil (see page 27), for ramekins

FOR THE CHOCOLATE SAUCE

½ cup heavy cream

2 ounces dark chocolate, broken into small pieces or finely chopped

---

If you wish to serve the panna cotta unmolded, increase the gelatin to 2¼ or 2½ teaspoons. To serve, spoon 2 tablespoons of chocolate sauce on each plate, then gently unmold the panna cotta on top.

Make the panna cotta: In a small dish, combine 2 tablespoons of water and the gelatin. Set aside to soak until dissolved.

Halve the vanilla bean lengthwise and scrape the seeds into a saucepan. Add the mint, sugar, milk, and cream. Bring almost to a simmer over low heat, stirring continuously and muddling the mint. Remove the mixture from the heat and allow it rest for about 10 minutes, but not longer.

Meanwhile, lightly oil four 5½-ounce ramekins.

Add the gelatin to the milk mixture and stir until dissolved. Strain the mixture into a pitcher or a mixing bowl with a spout. Divide it evenly among the prepared ramekins and cover loosely with plastic wrap. Chill in the refrigerator for at least 4 hours or overnight to set up.

Just before serving, make the chocolate sauce: Heat the cream in a small saucepan over low heat until very hot and steaming, but not boiling. Stir to prevent scalding. Place the chocolate in a small bowl. Pour the cream over the chocolate and allow it to sit for about 2 minutes to melt the chocolate, then stir until smooth.

To serve, spoon the chocolate sauce on top of each panna cotta in its ramekin. Serve immediately.

granita di caffè

COFFEE GRANITA

ROMAN SUMMERS are hot, with temperatures routinely exceeding 90°F. The unrelenting sun beats down on the city's cobblestones, which absorb heat by day and release it by night. Devoted coffee drinkers—and there are many—think twice about ordering an espresso. Even *caffè freddo*, a chilled sweetened espresso, isn't all that thirst quenching under such extreme conditions. That's when we reach for *granita di caffè*, a sweet coffee slush served layered with subtly sweet whipped cream.

makes 6 granite

FOR THE GRANITA

2 cups freshly brewed coffee, warm

5 tablespoons sugar

FOR THE WHIPPED CREAM

¾ cup heavy cream

3 tablespoons sugar

1 tablespoon Pernod

If you make the granita in advance, fluff the ice six to eight times as directed, then store it in the freezer. When you are ready to serve, remove it from the freezer 15 minutes ahead of time and scrape once more immediately before serving.

Make the granita: Combine the coffee and sugar in a medium bowl and allow to cool, about 20 minutes. Transfer the mixture to a rimmed baking sheet and place in the freezer for 30 minutes, until crystals begin to form. Scrape the crystals with a fork to break them up. Repeat this process every 15 minutes until the whole baking sheet has become fluffy ice, six to eight times.

Meanwhile, make the whipped cream: In a medium bowl, whip the cream until it starts to thicken. Add the sugar and Pernod, and continue to whip until soft peaks form.

Serve the granita in a juice or parfait glass, layering it with the whipped cream.

maritozzi con la panna

SWEET BUNS WITH WHIPPED CREAM

BEFORE THE ARRIVAL of industrial *cornetti*, the faux croissants that dominate breakfast offerings at Roman cafés, *maritozzi* reigned. These sweet, leavened buns originated as Lenten treats. Called *maritozzi quaresimali*, they incorporated pine nuts, raisins, and candied fruits. Our plain, simplified version is more common today; they are sliced opened and filled with barely sweetened whipped cream. At Regoli, a jewel of a historic bakery near Piazza Vittorio in the Esquiline district, *maritozzi* are displayed at the entrance, slathered with an amount of whipped cream that exceeds the width of the bun itself! This recipe yields our ideal *maritozzo*-to-whipped-cream ratio, but you be the judge. Bear in mind, you'll need to let the dough rise for 2 hours to find out.

makes 12 **maritozzi**

FOR THE SPONGE

½ cup warm milk (between 105°F and 115°F)

1¼ tablespoons active dry yeast

1 cup bread flour

1 tablespoon sugar

FOR THE DOUGH

7 tablespoons unsalted butter, at room temperature

½ cup sugar

⅛ teaspoon sea salt

4 large eggs, at room temperature

2½ cups bread flour, plus more for dusting

FOR THE EGG WASH

1 large egg

1 tablespoon whole milk

Make the sponge: In a medium bowl, whisk the yeast into the milk, then add the flour and sugar and stir to combine. Cover the mixture with plastic wrap and set aside until it becomes puffy, about 20 minutes.

Make the dough: In the bowl of a stand mixer fitted with the paddle attachment, combine the butter, sugar, salt, and eggs on low speed.

Replace the paddle with the dough hook. Pour in the sponge, mix for a few turns, then add half of the flour. Mix on low until the dough is smooth, about 5 minutes. Add the remaining flour and mix again on low until the dough is smooth, about 2 minutes, scraping down the sides of the bowl as necessary.

Allow the dough to rest in the bowl for 10 minutes, then run the mixer on low for 10 minutes to stretch the gluten. Meanwhile, line two rimmed baking sheets with parchment paper.

Turn the dough onto a lightly floured surface and divide it into twelve equal-size pieces (each approximately 2½ ounces). Using one hand, roll each piece into a tight ball, pressing it against the counter to ensure a smooth, tight surface. Next, using both hands, roll each ball into an elongated loaf shape, fatter in the middle and tapered on the ends, about 4 inches long, similar to a small football.

FOR THE FILLING

2 cups heavy cream

1 tablespoon sugar

Place *maritozzi* on the prepared baking sheets, spacing them
1½ inches apart. Cover with plastic wrap, then a kitchen towel,
and allow to rise in a warm place (between 70°F and 80°F) until
doubled in size, about 2 hours.

Preheat the oven to 350°F.

Make the egg wash: Whisk the egg with the milk in a small
bowl. Immediately before baking, brush the tops of the
maritozzi with the egg wash.

Bake until deep brown, 12 to 15 minutes. Remove from the
oven and allow to cool for 5 minutes on the baking sheet
before transferring to a wire rack.

While the *maritozzi* cool, make the filling: Whip the cream and
sugar to firm peaks.

Slice each *maritozzo* open without cutting all the way through.
Fill with the whipped cream, dividing it evenly, and serve
immediately.

crostata di prugne di sara levi

SARA LEVI'S PLUM *CROSTATA* WITH ALMOND CRUST

LATTICE-EMBELLISHED jam tarts called *crostate* turn up everywhere in Rome from breakfast tables and pastry shops to dessert spreads and cafés. Many are mass-produced and taste factory-made; few ever venture into the realm of exceptional. Our favorite version, made by pastry chef Sara Levi of the Rome Sustainable Food Project, certainly dwells in exceptional territory. Sara, a Roman American chef, takes cues from tradition, but also incorporates toasted almonds in her buttery crust for excellent texture and flavor.

makes one 9-inch crostata

1½ cups unblanched whole raw almonds

⅓ cup whole-wheat flour

1 cup all-purpose flour

½ teaspoon ground cinnamon

½ teaspoon sea salt

¾ cup (1½ sticks) unsalted butter, at room temperature, plus more for greasing

⅔ cup sugar

1 large egg yolk

1 cup plus 2 tablespoons plum jam

¼ cup sliced almonds (optional)

Preheat the oven to 320°F.

Spread the whole almonds out on a parchment paper–lined baking sheet and toast in the oven until fragrant, about 15 minutes. Remove and set aside to cool, about 30 minutes.

Combine the cooled almonds and the whole-wheat flour in a food processor and pulse until finely ground. Transfer to a medium bowl and add the all-purpose flour, cinnamon, and salt. Stir to combine and set aside.

In the bowl of a stand mixer fitted with the paddle attachment, beat the butter and sugar on medium speed until light and creamy, about 3 minutes. Scrape down the sides of the bowl with a rubber spatula, then add the egg yolk and beat on medium speed until incorporated. Add the flour mixture all at once and mix on low speed just until the dough begins to come together, not more than 1 minute. Scrape down the sides of the bowl and the paddle attachment with a rubber spatula and mix until the dough comes together, about 20 seconds more.

Gather the dough into a mass and divide it into two unequal pieces, about two-thirds and one-third. Wrap each piece in plastic wrap and chill in the refrigerator for 1 hour. (If you chill the dough longer, allow it to sit at room temperature for 30 minutes before using.)

Preheat the oven to 350°F. Lightly grease a 9-inch fluted tart pan or springform pan with butter.

Roll out the larger piece of dough between two lightly floured sheets of parchment paper to a thickness of between ¼ and ⅛ inch. Transfer it to the prepared pan, gently pressing it into the corners and up the sides; if you're using a springform pan, the dough should come about ¾ inch up the sides. Repair any tears. Refrigerate until firm, about 30 minutes.

Meanwhile, roll out the smaller piece of the dough the same way, then use a pastry wheel or sharp knife to cut it into 1-inch-wide strips. Freeze the strips until firm, about 5 minutes.

Remove the pan from the refrigerator, then spread the plum jam over the chilled crust. Create a simple lattice on top, or a woven lattice, if desired (see page 49). Trim any loose ends of the strips to fit the pan and pinch them to the edges of the bottom crust. Sprinkle over the sliced almonds (if using).

Bake until golden brown all over, about 40 minutes. Transfer to a wire rack to cool before unmolding, about 30 minutes. Serve immediately or wrap in aluminum foil and store at room temperature for up to 1 week.

torta di ricotta

SHEEP'S-MILK RICOTTA CHEESECAKE

THOUGH MENUS all over town call the local ricotta cake a
"cheesecake," it is a bit of a misnomer. Ricotta isn't technically cheese,
but rather the high-protein, high-fat by-product of cheese production.
In Rome, it is generally made from sheep's milk. Ricotta cake made with
sour cherry (*visciole*) jam is a classic of the Roman Jewish tradition and
similar to the *cassola* cheesecake that developed during the Ghetto period
(see page 106). Our no-bake cheesecake is inspired by the flavors of
the classic version. Remember you'll need to chill the cake for at least
4 hours or overnight before serving.

makes 1 torta di ricotta

FOR THE SPONGE CAKE

5 large eggs, separated

**½ cup plus 2 tablespoons
sugar**

**1 teaspoon pure vanilla
extract**

⅛ teaspoon sea salt

1 cup all-purpose flour

**Up to 3 tablespoons whole
milk, as needed**

FOR THE CHERRY
GLAZE AND FILLING

**1½ cups sour cherry
preserves**

**12 ounces ricotta (we like
sheep's-milk varieties)**

8 ounces cream cheese

½ cup sugar

**2 teaspoons pure vanilla
extract**

⅔ cup heavy cream

**Sour cherries (dried or
fresh), for garnish**

Make the sponge cake: Preheat the oven to 350°F. Line a 9-inch
springform pan with parchment paper.

In the bowl of a stand mixer fitted with the paddle attachment,
beat the egg yolks, sugar, and vanilla on medium speed until
the mixture is light yellow and fluffy and forms ribbons on the
surface when the paddle is lifted, about 4 minutes.

In a clean bowl of the stand mixer fitted with the whisk
attachment, combine the egg whites and salt and whisk on
medium speed until they form soft peaks.

Working in three batches, sift the flour over the egg yolk
mixture, delicately folding in each batch before adding the
next. Add about one-third of the egg whites and gently mix
to combine and loosen the batter. Fold in the rest of the
whites with a spatula, taking care not to deflate them. The
final batter should be of a dropping consistency. If the mixture
becomes pasty and dry, add up to 3 tablespoons whole milk, a
tablespoon at a time, to loosen it up.

Carefully transfer the mixture to the prepared pan and bake
until the cake has started to pull away from the sides and is
springy to the touch, about 30 minutes.

RECIPE CONTINUES

If you don't have a second mixer bowl, pour the egg mixture into a large bowl and wash and thoroughly dry the mixer bowl to proceed.

Remove the cake from the oven and allow to cool for 10 minutes before transferring to a rack to cool completely, about 45 minutes. Halve the cake horizontally. Return one layer, cut-side up, to a clean, parchment paper–lined springform pan. Wrap the other half in plastic wrap and refrigerate or freeze for another use.

Make the cherry glaze and filling: In a small pan, whisk two-thirds of the preserves with a little more than a tablespoon of water and cook over medium heat until the mixture becomes liquid, about 1 minute. Strain the preserves through a sieve into a small bowl and allow to cool for 5 minutes. Brush the sponge cake layer with the glaze, and set aside the remainder to use as a topping for the cheesecake.

In the bowl of a stand mixer fitted with the paddle attachment, mix the ricotta, cream cheese, sugar, and vanilla on medium speed until combined and fluffy. Gradually mix in the cream, then fold in the remaining cherry preserves.

To assemble the cheesecake: Pour the filling into the prepared pan over the sponge layer, smooth the top with an offset spatula, cover with plastic wrap, and chill in the refrigerator for at least 4 hours, or overnight.

Warm the reserved glaze with the sour cherries briefly on the stovetop. Pour the glaze and cherries over the cheesecake immediately before serving.

fave dei morti

DAY OF THE DEAD COOKIES

THE RITUAL of commemorating the dearly departed stretches back to time immemorial. Ancient Romans paid tribute on prescribed days, visiting tombs and even picnicking with their ancestors in the city's suburban cemeteries. These rituals were woven into Catholic ones and, while it is no longer a custom for Romans to bring food to the cemetery, they certainly do visit, with special bus services running to Prima Porta and Verano Cemeteries on November 2, All Souls' Day, called the *Commemorazione dei Defunti* or *Giorno dei Morti*. Bakeries in Rome mark the holiday with these special cookies called *fave dei morti*, fava beans of the dead.

makes 36 **fave dei morti**

1 heaping cup blanched almond flour

½ cup sugar

¾ cup plus 2 tablespoons all-purpose flour, plus more for dusting

2 teaspoons ground cinnamon

2 tablespoons unsalted butter, at room temperature

1 large egg

Preheat the oven to 350°F. Line a baking sheet with parchment paper.

In a medium bowl, mix all the ingredients together by hand to form a firm dough. Turn out onto a lightly floured surface and knead a couple of times, then halve. Roll each half into a small log about ¾ inch in diameter. Slice the log into 1-inch pieces and, with your thumb, make an indentation in the center of each. The indentation will resemble the shape of a fava bean.

Place these *fave* on the prepared baking sheet and bake for 12 to 15 minutes, until dry and just beginning to brown. Remove from the oven and allow to cool completely on the baking sheet, about 30 minutes. They will be soft when they come out of the oven but will harden as they cool.

brutti ma buoni

HAZELNUT MERINGUES

BRUTTI MA BUONI, "ugly but delicious," is a phrase perfectly suited to much of Rome's food. The ingredients may be gorgeous, but the finished product is often aesthetically challenged. In this case, *brutti ma buoni* specifically refers to meringues loaded with chopped toasted hazelnuts. They are sold by weight at traditional bakeries like Antico Forno Roscioli and Forno Campo de' Fiori. Trust us—the beauty of these is in the taste.

makes 30 **brutti ma buoni**

10 ounces raw hazelnuts, skin on

5 ounces egg whites (from about 5 large eggs)

Large pinch of sea salt

2½ cups confectioners' sugar, sifted

1 teaspoon pure vanilla extract

Preheat the oven to 350°F. Spread the hazelnuts on a rimmed baking sheet and toast in the oven for 8 to 10 minutes, or until the skins begin to crack and loosen. Remove from the oven and allow to cool until they can be handled, about 10 minutes, then rub them with a clean tea towel to mostly remove the skins.

Reduce the oven temperature to 300°F. Line a baking sheet with parchment paper.

In a food processor, pulse the hazelnuts until the pieces are small, but not quite fine.

In the bowl of a stand mixer fitted with the wire whisk, whip the egg whites and salt on medium speed until foamy. With the mixer running, gradually add the sugar in a steady stream, continuing to whisk until the mixture appears glossy and starts to thicken. Fold in the hazelnuts and vanilla.

Transfer the mixture to a heavy-bottomed medium saucepan. Cook over low heat, stirring continuously with a wooden spoon, until the mixture begins to dry out and clump somewhat, comes away from the sides of the pan, and begins to turn beige, about 10 minutes. Remove the pan from the heat. Working quickly, use two spoons to place mounds of the batter on the prepared baking sheet, spacing them 1½ inches apart.

Bake for about 15 minutes, until lightly browned. The cookie will feel a bit soft when pressed but will harden on the outside when cool. Serve immediately or store in an aluminum cookie tin at room temperature for up to 2 weeks.

DRINKS

Few places are as inextricably linked to wine as Rome is. The ancient city was responsible for introducing vines and viticulture to every corner of its empire. It's no wonder young Romans view wine as old-fashioned, turning many to cocktails and craft beer instead. In the past few years, cocktail culture has blossomed. We asked our favorite bartenders to share their signature drinks to show just how far Rome has come. Think of making cocktails like baking: proportions count. For that reason, it's best to make these one at a time.

carbonara sour di co.so.

CO.SO.'S CARBONARA SOUR

AFTER FIFTEEN YEARS behind the bar at the five-star luxury Hotel de Russie, Massimo D'Addezio left to open his own cocktail bar, Co.So. Cocktail & Social in Pigneto, eastern Rome's nightlife epicenter. With the support and skills of London-trained bartender Giorgia Crea, Co.So. does a brisk business of cocktails that are twists on the classics, with cheeky names like the Carbonara Sour. Our version is a fresh and light vodka sour with black pepper and citrus introducing a little kick and a mellow savoriness from the *guanciale*-washed (fat-infused) vodka. You can make this drink right away with plain vodka, but the *guanciale* version is worth the time and effort.

makes 1 cocktail

2 ounces *Guanciale-Washed Vodka* (recipe follows)

¾ ounce Simple Syrup (page 233)

¾ ounce fresh lemon juice

1 egg white

Lemon twist

Pinch of freshly ground black pepper

Combine the vodka, simple syrup, lemon juice, and egg white in a shaker. Dry shake without ice for around 15 seconds. Add ice to fill the shaker and shake vigorously until well chilled, 30 seconds.

Strain into a rocks glass over ice. Garnish with a lemon twist and a pinch of black pepper.

vodka al guanciale

GUANCIALE-WASHED VODKA

makes 1 pint guanciale-*washed vodka*

2 cups 80- or 100-proof vodka

½ cup rendered *guanciale* fat (see page 71)

Combine the vodka and *guanciale* fat in a medium jar and shake well. Place in the freezer for at least 36 hours. The fat should separate and rise to the top.

Remove from the freezer, discard the fat, and carefully pour off the vodka through a fine-mesh strainer or several layers of cheesecloth. Store in the refrigerator for up to 1 week.

ROMAN PUB CULTURE

BEER CULTURE runs deep in central Italy; long before the city's founding fathers Romulus and Remus allegedly washed up on the Tiber banks in what later became Rome, the nearby Etruscan tribes were consuming a grain-based, honey-laced fermented beverage they called *pevakh*. Later, as Rome expanded into that neighboring territory, the Romans dabbled in brewing, too. But beer never challenged the dominance of wine and remained largely a lower-class tipple.

Beer production waned in the Middle Ages and wasn't revived in a significant way until the Peroni factory was built near Porta Pia north of the center in 1901. For most of the next century, industrial beers ruled Rome, unchallenged by craft options until these types of pubs began cropping up in the late nineties. Drawing from the British model, they emphasized beer over food, a choice that relegated them to the fringes of Rome's drinking culture, which posits alcohol and food as equal partners. Still, places like Le Bon Bock in the Gianicolense district and Mastro Titta in the Ostiense neighborhood gained small but loyal followings, paving the way for the first craft beer pub in central Rome: Manuele Colonna's Ma Che Siete Venuti a Fà (Macchè to regulars) in the heart of Trastevere.

Colonna's motto, *Quanno moro vojo esse fermentato*, is a tongue-in-cheek request in the local dialect: "When I die I want to be fermented." The craft beer game is high stakes for this pub owner, whose bar and the cobblestones outside are packed day and night. Macchè thrives in one of the city's most popular nightlife destinations, where Heineken and Corona are as popular as Peroni and Nastro Azzurro. The beers from its dozen or so taps, poured from behind a small wooden bar, range from vintage Italian sour ales to obscure Franconian lagers. Colonna and his pub are ambassadors for a different way of drinking and, without Macchè, it's unlikely craft beer would ever have become so popular in Rome.

Today, Colonna's craft beer evangelizing is just one voice in a chorus of many who have opened quality pubs and beer shops in Rome. Places like Stavio, Open Baladin, and no.au, all owned by brewers, champion Italian craft brews as food-friendly alternatives to wine. At these venues and dozens of others that have opened in recent years, potato croquettes, burgers, and even desserts engineered to match the beers on tap attract a wider clientele. A pub serving meals is akin to a wine bar serving small plates, and both scenarios appeal to young Romans in search of new flavors and economical dining options. Craft beer may never be the first beverage you associate with Rome, but if the nightly crowds outside Open Baladin and Macchè are any indication, its popularity shows no signs of letting up.

cinquième arrondissement
del gin corner

THE HOTEL ADRIANO near the Italian Parliament inaugurated The Gin Corner, a cocktail bar, in its lobby in the summer of 2013. With just fifty labels, it had the largest gin collection in all of Italy at the time. Now its list has reached more than eighty-five and the bar has become a point of reference for local and visiting connoisseurs alike. Obviously, the bar specializes in gin & tonics and martinis, but the house cocktail is a tart gin sour finished with a splash of red wine for color and structure. If you prefer drinks that weigh in on the sweet side, use rich simple syrup instead (see below).

makes 1 cocktail

1½ ounces London dry gin (we like Beefeater)

¾ ounce elderflower liqueur (we like St-Germain)

¾ ounce Simple Syrup (recipe follows)

¾ ounce fresh lemon juice

1 egg white

¼ ounce red wine (we like Montepulciano d'Abruzzo or Cesanese)

Combine the gin, elderflower liqueur, simple syrup, lemon juice, and egg white in a metal shaker. Dry shake with the metal coil from a Hawthorne strainer for 15 to 20 seconds.

Add ice to the shaker and shake vigorously for another 15 to 20 seconds. Strain into an empty shaker with no ice and dry shake vigorously for 15 to 20 seconds more.

Transfer to a Collins glass with ice and, using a bar spoon, gently float the red wine by pouring it over the back of the spoon in the center of the glass. Given its weight, the wine will automatically sink below the foam, creating a pretty layered effect.

sciroppo di zucchero

SIMPLE SYRUP

makes 1 cup simple syrup (1:1) or rich simple syrup (2:1)

1 to 2 cups sugar

In a small saucepan, combine 1 cup (for regular simple syrup) or 2 cups (for rich simple syrup) sugar and 1 cup water. Heat over medium-high heat, stirring, until the sugar has dissolved, 3 to 4 minutes.

Remove from the heat and set aside to cool, about 20 minutes. Store in a sealed jar in the refrigerator for up to 1 week.

cosa nostra di patrick pistolesi

PATRICK PISTOLESI'S COSA NOSTRA

NOT TO BE confused with the Sicilian mafia, which is far more potent than any libation, this drink is the house cocktail at Caffè Propaganda near the Colosseum. Its creator, Patrick Pistolesi, one of the pioneers in Rome's contemporary cocktail scene, is an Irish Italian barman with a flair for American and Italian classics. Here, he merges these two strengths, mixing a sort of Italian Old-Fashioned. Bourbon is the base, joined by the Italian bitter liqueurs Campari, Rabarbaro Zucca, and Fernet Branca.

makes 1 cocktail

¼ ounce Simple Syrup (page 233)

1 bar spoon Campari

1 bar spoon Rabarbaro Zucca

2 dashes of Fernet Branca

1½ ounces bourbon

Lemon twist

In a mixing glass filled with ice, combine the simple syrup, Campari, Rabarbaro Zucca, Fernet Branca, and bourbon. Stir until chilled, about 30 seconds.

Pour into an Old-Fashioned glass filled with one large ice cube. Twist a strip of lemon peel over the glass and drop it in to garnish.

frida kahlo

IN 2014, from March until August, the echoing halls of the Scuderie del Quirinale, a museum based in the former papal horse stables, hosted an exhibition on Mexican surrealist artist Frida Kahlo. At the time, Pino Mondello, a Sicily native and longtime fixture on the Roman cocktail scene, was developing the drinks list for Litro, a cocktail bar in the Monteverde Vecchio neighborhood. This drink, an homage to Kahlo, was created after he visited the exhibition and left inspired by the artist's 1939 journey to France. The Frida Kahlo blends the Mexican spirit Ilegal Joven mezcal with Lillet and St-Germain for a smoky and floral effect.

makes 1 cocktail

1¾ ounces mezcal (we like Ilegal Joven)

1 ounce Lillet

¾ ounce elderflower liqueur (we like St-Germain)

Half an orange slice

Pour the mezcal, Lillet, and elderflower liqueur over ice in a rocks glass. Stir until chilled, about 30 seconds.

Garnish with half an orange slice.

nerone

NERO

THE ROMAN EMPEROR Nero is perhaps best known for a fictitious event: fiddling from a tower as he watched Rome burn in the devastating fire of AD 64. Before committing suicide four years later, the emperor had earned a reputation for his obsession with drama and spectacle, which he enjoyed in private theaters and public stadiums. Giorgia Crea has captured Nero's absurdity in her chariot-drawn Nerone cocktail at Co.So. Cocktail & Social in Pigneto, which she serves with smoldering bay leaves in a chariot-led cup. A veteran of Rome's Hotel de Russie and London's bar scene, she is known for mixing whimsical twists on the classics, and for original inventions that tap the flavors of her native Rome. In this cocktail, the bitter and medicinal flavors of gentian root liqueur mingle with the herbaceous bay leaf infusion, all of which are softened by the corn-based bourbon. You'll need to make the vodka in advance, but the good news is you'll have some leftover to mix with club soda or tonic.

makes I cocktail

¼ ounce gentian root liqueur (we like Suze)

¼ ounce Simple Syrup (page 233)

½ ounce Bay Leaf–Infused Vodka (recipe follows)

1½ ounces bourbon (we like Buffalo Trace)

Wash a rocks glass with gentian root liqueur and discard excess spirit. Add the simple syrup, bay leaf infusion, bourbon, and one large ice cube to the glass and stir until chilled.

vodka all'alloro

BAY LEAF-INFUSED VODKA

makes I pint vodka all'alloro

2 cups 80- or 100-proof vodka

10 fresh or dried bay leaves, crumbled

In a medium jar, combine the vodka and bay leaves. Seal and allow the bay leaves to infuse the vodka for at least 48 hours. Remove the bay leaves and store in the refrigerator.

spritz con cynar

CYNAR SPRITZ

A SPRITZ is a popular apéritif that blends sparkling wine, soda, and a bitter red Italian liqueur such as Campari, Aperol, or Select. Our twist on the classic Spritz uses Cynar, an artichoke-based liqueur, which mirrors the sweet earthiness of Rome's native artichoke varieties. The result is a light, pleasant apéritif with balanced bitter and sweet notes.

makes 1 cocktail

2 ounces Prosecco or dry sparkling wine

1 ounce club soda

1½ ounces Cynar

Lemon slice

Pour the Prosecco, club soda, and Cynar into a highball glass over ice.

Serve garnished with a lemon slice.

garibaldi

THE GARIBALDI

EVERY ITALIAN TOWN has a piazza dedicated to General Giuseppe Garibaldi. In Rome, the square occupies a commanding position at the apex of the Janiculum Hill and provides unparalleled views of beauty over Rome's skyline and St. Peter's cupola, a supremely symbolic expression of Garibaldi's conquest of Rome in 1870. If there were a hilltop bar up there, we'd order this twist on the classic Garibaldi cocktail, a drink that calls for equal parts orange juice and Campari; we prefer a 2:1 combo in favor of blood orange juice. On the hot days when we crave bubbles, we'd add a splash of Prosecco, too.

makes 1 cocktail

1 ounce Prosecco or dry sparkling wine (optional)

2 ounces fresh blood orange juice or regular orange juice

1 ounce Campari

Orange slice

Pour the Prosecco (if using), orange juice, and Campari into a highball glass over ice.

Serve garnished with an orange slice.

digestivo all'alloro

BAY LAUREL DIGESTIF

THIS DIGESTIF is inspired by Alfredo Bergamini, one of the last remaining fishermen to work on the Tiber River. Alfredo makes a huge range of digestifs, plucking fennel flowers, bay leaves, and other spontaneous herbs from the property around his dock. He steeps fresh bay leaves in alcohol, then combines them with simple syrup, serving his potent potable after meals and extolling the digestive qualities of his homemade brew. Alfredo's *Digestivo all'Alloro* takes about 7 weeks altogether to make, so it requires some patience, but it's super simple and a fun thing to break out at the end of a dinner party. For the sake of digestion, of course.

makes 8 cups

4 cups (1 liter) Everclear 190 Proof

60 fresh bay leaves, washed and crumpled

4 cups (1 liter) water

5 cups (1 kilogram) sugar

Place the alcohol and bay leaves in a large glass jar. Seal and keep in a dark place for 40 days. Agitate the jar every few days.

On the last day, heat the water and sugar together in a large saucepan over medium-high heat. Meanwhile, strain the infused alcohol into another jar, discarding the bay leaves. When the sugar has dissolved, 3 to 4 minutes, remove the pan from the heat and allow the syrup to cool, about 20 minutes.

Add three-quarters of the syrup to the jar with the alcohol. Adjust the sweetness to taste, adding more syrup as needed. Allow the liquid to rest for 1 week in the closed jar in a dark place at room temperature.

Serve very cold or over ice. The digestif will keep for at least 6 months in the fridge and well over a year in the freezer in a sealed container.

martinez romano

ROMAN MARTINEZ

THE GIN MARTINEZ is a pre-Prohibition cocktail first presented by America's earliest celebrity bartender, Jerry Thomas, also known as "The Professor." Back in the day, he mixed Old Tom Gin, sweet vermouth, Maraschino liqueur, and orange bitters to create a cocktail he called The Martinez. Our version is adapted from his namesake bar, The Jerry Thomas Project, which uses their own Vermouth del Professore Classico Bianco, a moscato-based wine, fortified with alcohol and aromatized with more than a dozen herbs and spices. The vermouth has made quite a splash abroad, and you can find it at stores in the United States.

makes 1 cocktail

1½ ounces gin (for a drier version, we like Beefeater; for a sweeter version we like Old Tom)

1½ ounces Vermouth del Professore Classico Bianco

¼ ounce Maraschino liqueur

2 dashes of orange bitters

2 dashes of Angostura bitters

Lemon twist

Combine the gin, vermouth, Maraschino, orange bitters, and Angostura bitters in a chilled mixing glass with ice. Stir until chilled, about 30 seconds, then strain into a chilled cocktail glass or coupe.

Twist a strip of lemon peel over the glass and drop it in to garnish.

mex man del jerry thomas project

THE JERRY THOMAS PROJECT'S MEX MAN

MEZCAL, a smoky Mexican spirit, has seen a global revival recently. Just a few years ago, a decent bottle was hard to come by in Rome—and elsewhere. Now any cocktail bar worth its salt stocks a wide range of tequila's moody cousin. At The Jerry Thomas Project speakeasy in central Rome, mezcal is combined with one of their own fortified wines, Vermouth del Professore Rosso, an artisanal product made in the historic style of Turin. This vermouth, which is now available in the United States, lends a pleasant herbal earthiness to the subtly smoky drink.

makes 1 cocktail

1½ ounces mezcal

1½ ounces vermouth di Torino (we like Vermouth del Professore Rosso)

1 bar spoon agave syrup

2 dashes of chocolate bitters

2 dashes of orange bitters

Mezcal-Flavored Cherries (recipe follows)

Combine the mezcal, vermouth, agave syrup, chocolate bitters, and orange bitters in a mixing glass filled with ice and stir until chilled, about 30 seconds. Strain into a chilled coupette.

Serve garnished with a few mezcal-flavored cherries skewered on a toothpick.

ciliegie al mezcal

MEZCAL-FLAVORED CHERRIES

makes 1½ cups ciliegie al mezcal

1½ cups fresh, pitted cherries

2 tablespoons unground coffee beans

¾ cup mezcal

¾ cup Rich Simple Syrup (page 233)

Fill a medium jar with the cherries and coffee beans. Top with the mezcal and rich simple syrup. Seal the jar, shake to combine, and store for 1 month in a dark place before using.

AN ECCENTRIC PRINCE
AND HIS ROMAN VINEYARD

FOR MOST of the twentieth century, much of the wine made in
Rome's environs was praised for its simplicity or value and not much
was even remotely prestigious. There was, however, a major exception:
the spectacular age-worthy wines made by one eccentric prince and his
small team of farmers.

Near the tenth milestone of the Via Appia, the ancient highway
stretching 350 miles from Rome to the Adriatic Sea, Prince Alberico
Boncompagni Ludovisi, a descendant of papal royalty, transformed his
country estate into a bastion of unparalleled quality. Next to crumbling
imperial ruins, the prince coaxed complexity and minerality from his
grapes to produce wines under the Fiorano label.

Fiorano's legacy was built upon a bold and unorthodox act. The
prince pulled up many of the indigenous vines on his property and
replaced them with Merlot, Cabernet Sauvignon, and Semillon from
France. The only local grape he deemed worthy was Malvasia di Candia.

For half a century, the prince ignored the local wine fashions and
instead made the kind of wines he wanted to drink. They garnered
a cult following and, although they relied on French grapes, were
profoundly personal, completely influenced by him, and therefore
undeniably Roman.

Few Romans had the privilege to drink or the access to Fiorano.
The prince infamously sold his wine directly from the vineyard office,
a stucco structure dubbed "L'Amministrazione," set just off Via Appia.
Transactions were quirky—he refused to make change and wouldn't
necessarily fill the order as the client had requested and paid for—but
his customers were hooked and put up with the antics.

After the 1995 harvest, in failing health, the prince tore up most
of his vineyards. Many suspect he didn't trust anyone to respect his
winemaking legacy. Then in 2000 he brokered a deal to sell off
the contents of his cellar, dispersing the finest wines Rome has ever
produced and ensuring that you are more likely to find the prince's
wines on a high-end Italian restaurant menu in New York than in the
city of their birth.

acknowledgments

First and foremost, thank you to our editor and biggest advocate, Amanda Englander, who believed in our book from day one and immediately embraced our vision of Rome. The whole team at Clarkson Potter is amazing, so *grazie infinite* to Doris Cooper, Anna Mintz, Carly Gorga, Lauren Velasquez, Stephanie Huntwork, Terry Deal, and Luisa Francavilla. Thank you also to our publisher, Aaron Wehner, whose wealth of experience has enabled us to craft a book of which we are truly proud. We are boundlessly appreciative to Alison Fargis, our agent, who shepherded us through it all. Our recipe testers, Tatiana Perea, Brad Spence, and Talia Baiocchi, provided invaluable insight and advice. A very special thanks to Matt Armendariz, Adam C. Pearson, and their entire team at Shooter+Stylist.

This book would not exist in its current form without the generous collaboration of Rome's chefs, restaurateurs, *pizzaioli*, *gelatai*, bakers, butchers, eel fishermen, craft beer evangelists, wine makers, and bartenders who recounted their stories, opened their kitchens, and shared their recipes with enthusiasm. Flavio De Maio, Claudio Torcè, the Gargioli family, Stefano Callegari, Francesca Barreca, Marco Baccanelli, the Sartor family, Sergio and Mara Esposito, Maria Agnese Spagnuolo, Leonardo Vignoli, Maria Pia Cicconi, the Roscioli family, Gabriele Bonci, Daniele Crescenzi, Alessandro Fanelli and Az. Ag. Fanelli, Vito Bernabei, Umberto Pavoncello, the Rome Sustainable Food Project kitchen, Principe Alessandrojacopo Boncompagni Ludovisi and the Tenuta di Fiorano, Patrick Pistolesi, Giorgia Crea, Valerio Albrizio, Massimo D'Addezio, The Jerry Thomas Project (a special shout-out to Simona for her infinite patience), Federico Tomaselli, Pino Mondello and the Litro crew, Manuele Colonna, La Tradizione, and Cesare and Alfredo Bergamini, *vi ringraziamo di cuore*.

KATIE WOULD LIKE TO THANK

Chris Behr, a constant source of inspiration and wisdom and the person to whom I owe my greatest debt of gratitude; John Regefalk, whose advice and friendship carried me through this project and whose generosity is rivaled only by his baking prowess; Sara Levi for her tireless support, expert advice, and sweetness.

Thanks also to Jo Ann Parla, Lauren Parla, Papa Parla, Nonno Cipollina, Mario Batali, Andrew Zimmern, Mark Bittman, Dana Cowin, Jessica Stewart, Hande and Theo Leimer, Kat Tan Conte, Andrew Sessa, Brian Sandstrom, Rachel Roddy, Maureen Fant, Şemsa Denizsel,

Cenk Sönmezsoy, Ruth Lo, Nathaniel Rich, Sarah Johnson, Ned Maddock, the Vetri Family, Jack Kukoda, Coach G, and Beth Feehan for their continual help, guidance, support, and snacks.

KRISTINA WOULD LIKE TO THANK

My husband, Niccolò, for being dedicated to every aspect of my contribution from photo assisting to prop sourcing to photo scouting; Matt Armendariz, for being himself—I would never have gotten this far without him; Grace Bonney for entrusting me with the "In the Kitchen with" column at Design*Sponge way back when; my tireless PA, Jennice Torres; Sam Beever for celebrating every deadline with me; Bryant Terry for his insight; Tag Christof for checking in on me daily; Flavio Girolami for explaining the key to success; Samina Langholz and Andrea Brugi for their beautiful wood props; and Michael Nagin for pushing my photography to the next level.

Thanks also to Alessandra, Baby Alice, Ana, Angela, Angelique, Aran, Carolina, Deb and Paul, Daniele, Francesca, Harriet, Heidi, Hilda, Hristina, Jennifer, Jocelyn, Joe, Johnny, Julia, Justin, Kerrbear, Laura, Leela, Lexi, Luisa, Mary, Matt Lewis, Neale, Nicole, Peter, Rashad, Sam S., Sarah R., Sasha at Farm Lot 59, Shelley, Stie, Talmadge, Tom, Yashica, and Yvette B, for their moral support and enthusiasm; to my family for their enduring belief in me; and to my Savoir Bed for perfect sleep every night after very long days in the city that has been my home for sixteen years.

bibliography

Agnetti, Vittorio. *La Nuova Cucina delle Specialità Regionali.* Milan: Società Editoriale Milanese, 1909.

Boni, Ada. *Il Talismano della Felicità.* Rome: Colombo, 2006.

Boni, Ada. *La Cucina Romana.* Rome: New Compton Editori, 2010.

Boswell, Christopher, and Elena Goldblatt. *Verdure: Recipes from the Kitchen of the American Academy in Rome.* New York: Little Bookroom, 2014.

Cato, Marcus Porcius, and Andrew Dalby. *On Farming De Agricultura.* Devon: Prospect Books, 1998.

Cougnet, Dr. Alberto. *Il Ventre dei Popoli Saggi Di Cucine Etniche e Nazionali.* Turin: Fratelli Bocca, 1905.

Dalby, Andrew. *The Classical Cookbook.* London: British Museum Press, 1996.

Dandini, Arcangelo. *Animelle: Viaggio di un Oste.* Rome: IniziativeItalia, 2014.

Dandini, Arcangelo. *Memorie a Mozzichi.* Reggio Emilia: Alberti Editore, 2011.

Di Nepi, Serena. *Sopravvivere al Ghetto: per una storia sociale della comunità ebraica nella Roma del Cinquecento.* Rome: Viella, 2013.

Ferré, M. Cécile, Mauruzio, Maurizi, and Teresa Di Marco. *La Cucina di Roma e del Lazio.* Milan: Guido Tommasi Editore, 2012.

Gargioli, Claudio. *Menù Letterario Tipico Romano: Recipes and Love from our Roman Kitchen.* Rome: Atmosphere Libri, 2014.

Goldstein, Joyce. *Cucina Ebraica: Flavors of the Italian Jewish Kitchen.* San Francisco: Chronicle Books, 1998.

Murray, Trevor. *Pliny the Elder's Natural History: The Empire in the Encyclopedia.* Oxford: Oxford University Press, 2004.

Peña, J. Theodore. *Roman Pottery in the Archaeological Record.* Cambridge: Cambridge University Press, 2007.

Roden, Claudia. *The Book of Jewish Food: An Odyssey from Samarkand to New York.* New York: Knopf, 1996.

Roumani, Maurice. *The Jews of Libya.* Brighton: Sussex Academic Press, 2009.

Scully, Terrence. *The Opera of Bartolomeo Scappi.* Toronto: University of Toronto Press, 2011.

Stow, Kenneth R. *Jewish Life in Early Modern Rome: Challenge, Conversion, and Private Life.* Farnum: Ashgate, 2007.

Stow, Kenneth R. *The Jews in Rome.* Leiden: E.J. Brill, 1995.

Toaff, Ariel. *Mangiare alla Giudia: La cucina ebraica in Italia del Rinascimento all'età moderna.* Bologna: Il Mulino, 2000.

Waagenaar, Sam. *Il Ghetto sul Tevere.* Milan: Arnoldo Mondadori Editore, 1973.

Ward-Perkins, Bryan. *The Fall of Rome: And the End of Civilization.* Oxford: Oxford University Press, 2005.

Zanini De Vita, Oretta. *Encyclopedia of Pasta.* Translated by Mauren Fant. Oakland: University of California Press, 2009.

Zanini De Vita, Oretta. *Il Lazio a Tavola.* Rome: Alphabyte Books, 1994.

Zanini De Vita, Oretta. *Popes, Peasants, and Shepherds: Recipes and Lore from Rome and Lazio.* Translated by Mauren Fant. Oakland: University of California Press, 2013.

Zanini De Vita, Oretta, and Maureen Fant. *Sauces & Shapes: Pasta the Italian Way.* New York: W. W. Norton, 2013.

resources

FOOD

Anson Mills
803-467-4122
ansonmills.com
For organic heirloom wheat
flours.

**Benton's Smoky
Mountain Country Ham**
423-442-5003
bentonscountryhams2.com
This fine producer of country
ham also makes *guanciale*,
Call to order; it isn't listed on
their site.

Bluebird Grain Farms
509-996-3526
bluebirdgrainfarms.com
For emmer flour and other
quality grains milled to order.

Boccalone
415-433-6500
boccalone.com
For *guanciale*, *lardo*, and
'nduja.

Buon Italia
212-633-9090
buonitalia.com
For flours, pasta, salted
anchovies, cheese, *guanciale*,
bottarga, and assorted Italian
specialties.

Creminelli
801-428-1820
creminelli.com
For *corallina*-style salami.

Di Bruno Brothers
888-322-4337
For Pecorino Romano,
Parmigiano-Reggiano,
Gorgonzola, sheep's-milk
ricotta, mozzarella, and other
Italian cheese, as well as
guanciale.

Eataly
212-539-0833
eataly.com
Pastas, cured meats, cheeses,
rice, and a variety of Italian
products.

Formaggio Kitchen
888-212-3224
formaggiokitchen.com
For *guanciale*, cheeses,
pastas, olive oils, and other
specialty products.

Fra' Mani
510-526-7000
framani.com
For *corallina*-style salami.

Heritage Foods
718-389-0985
heritagefoodsusa.com
For caul fat.

King Arthur Flour
800-827-6836
kingarthurflour.com
For quality flours.

Local Harvest
831-515-5602
localharvest.org
A network of local farms
for sourcing fresh pork jowl
for *guanciale*, among other
things.

Market Hall Foods
510-250-6006
markethallfoods.com
For fennel pollen, salted
anchovies, and a wide range
of Italian specialty products.

Murray's
888-692-4339
murrayscheese.com
For *guanciale*, *'nduja*,
cheeses, and Italian specialty
products of all kinds.

Rancho Gordo
707-259-1935
ranchogordo.com
For *borlotti* (cranberry
beans).

Salumeria Biellese
212-736-7376
salumeriabiellese.com
For *guanciale* and *'nduja*.

Zingerman's
888-636-8162
zingermans.com
For *guanciale*, *lardo*, *'nduja*,
cheeses, and a huge variety of
Italian specialty products.

UTENSILS

Bar Products
800-BLOODY-MARY
(256-6396)
barproducts.com
For cocktail tools of all kinds.

Cocktail Kingdom
212-647-9166
cocktailkingdom.com
For professional cocktail
accessories and tools.

JB Prince
212-683-3553
jbprince.com
Baking sheets, terrine molds,
baking utensils, and kitchen
equipment.

OXO
oxo.com
800-545-4411
Good, sturdy cooking and
baking utensils.

Sur La Table
800-243-0852
surlatable.com
High-end cookwear, sturdy
pots, and pizza stones.

Williams-Sonoma
877-812-6235
williams-sonoma.com
For cookware, bakeware,
baking stones, cocktail tools,
ice cream makers, ice cube
trays, and assorted baking
tools.

conversions

WEIGHT

US	METRIC
½ ounce	14.2 grams
1 ounce	28.3 grams
1 pound (16 ounces)	453 grams
2.2 pounds	1 kilogram

SOME SAMPLE WEIGHTS

	MEASURE	WEIGHT (GRAMS)
All-purpose flour	1 cup	about 125 grams
Bread flour	1 cup	about 140 grams
Extra-virgin olive oil	1 tablespoon	about 14 grams
Salt	1 teaspoon	about 6 grams
Granulated sugar	1 cup	about 200 grams
Grated Parmigiano-Reggiano	1 ounce	28.3 grams
Grated Pecorino Romano	1 ounce	28.3 grams

LIQUID VOLUME

1 teaspoon = 4.9 milliliters
1 tablespoon = 3 teaspoons = 14.7 milliliters
1 cup = 237 milliliters
2 cups = 1 pint = 474 milliliters
4 cups = 1 quart = 948 milliliters
4.22 cups = 1 liter

LENGTH

1 inch = 2.5 centimeters
1 centimeter = .4 inches

index